Social Issues in Literature

P9-AQQ-297

Violence in William Golding's *Lord of the Flies*

Dedria Bryfonski, Book Editor

GREENHAVEN PRESS
A part of Gale, Cengage Learning

GALE
CENGAGE Learning™

Detroit • New York • San Francisco • New Haven, Conn • Waterville, Maine • London

Christine Nasso, *Publisher*
Elizabeth Des Chenes, *Managing Editor*

For more information, contact:
Greenhaven Press
27500 Drake Rd.
Farmington Hills, MI 48331-3535
Or you can visit our Internet site at gale.cengage.com

For product information and technology assistance, contact us at

Gale Customer Support, 1-800-877-4253
For permission to use material from this text or product, submit all requests online at www.cengage.com/permissions

Further permissions questions can be emailed to permissionrequest@cengage.com

Articles in Greenhaven Press anthologies are often edited for length to meet page requirements. In addition, original titles of these works are changed to clearly present the main thesis and to explicitly indicate the author's opinion. Every effort is made to ensure that Greenhaven Press accurately reflects the original intent of the authors. Every effort has been made to trace the owners of copyrighted material.

Cover image © Photos 12/Alamy.

LIBRARY OF CONGRESS CATALOGING-IN-PUBLICATION DATA

Violence in William Golding's Lord of the flies / Dedria Bryfonski, book editor.
    p. cm. -- (Social issues in literature)
    Includes bibliographical references and index.
    ISBN 978-0-7377-4618-1 (hardcover)
    ISBN 978-0-7377-4619-8 (pbk.)
    1. Golding, William, 1911-1993. Lord of the flies. 2. Violence in literature.
    3. Boys in literature. I. Bryfonski, Dedria.
    PR6013.O35L647 2009
    823'.914--dc22
                                                                    2009018941

Printed in the United States of America
1 2 3 4 5 6 7 13 12 11 10 09

Social Issues
in Literature

Violence in William
Golding's *Lord of the Flies*

Other Books in the Social Issues in Literature Series:

Contents

Chapter 2: Violence in *Lord of the Flies*

Chapter 3: Contemporary Perspectives on Violence

Introduction

William Golding could hardly be termed an overnight success as a novelist. He is a self-professed "very late developer." It was not for want of trying. He began writing at the age of seven and had a book of poetry, called *Poems*, published when he was twenty-three. Although he continued to write, it would be two decades before his next book, *Lord of the Flies*, saw print. During that time, Golding wrote three unpublished novels he called "pot-boilers" that were largely derivative. Finally, he claims he learned during that time the "one great truth: that I have to write my own books, not anyone else's."

Golding found his voice and theme in the horrific experiences of World War II. The war had a profound effect on the twentieth century and on the authors whose careers were shaped by their wartime experiences. For Golding, World War II would shatter his previously held views about the perfectibility of human society.

"When I was young, before the War, I did have some airy-fairy views about man. . . . But I went through the war and that changed me," Golding stated. Golding became preoccupied with the problem of evil. His experiences in the war taught him that evil is inherent in human nature and can emerge at any time. And in any place.

Golding's wartime experiences were of two kinds, and both would prove to be formative. The first were personal experiences. The second, and even more compelling, according to his daughter, Judy Carver, and writer Kevin McCarron, were the postwar revelations of the atrocities committed in the Holocaust. Golding concluded that the horrors perpetrated by the Nazis could have happened anywhere, because both good and evil are innate in human nature.

Golding was drafted into service in the British Royal Navy following the outbreak of World War II and rose to the rank of lieutenant. As the captain of a rocket-launching ship, participant in D-Day and in the sinking of the giant German warship the *Bismarck*, Golding was in the thick of the activities during World War II. Two events in particular have been cited as influential in darkening his view of human behavior.

His experiences leading up to D-Day were life-changing, according to his friend, the writer and historian Andrew Sinclair:

> He went out on D-Day, this huge embargo, the biggest ever seen. And his ship was very slow. It was also a tinderbox. One tracer bullet, the whole thing went. These were probably the most dangerous ships in the navy, they were wood and they were just full of explosives. Anyway, he went to sleep and left the ship to his first mate and they had missed the whole of the D-Day flotilla. It had just disappeared. So what was he to do? It was the worst moment of his life. Ahead of him lay a minefield. Marked on the charts. If he went across the minefield he'd get to D-Day on time and kill his quotient of Germans. If he didn't, and went around, he'd miss the whole of D-Day. So he took the decision to go across the minefield. So he went across the minefield. He lay opposite the beaches of Normandy and lobbed in his two hundred bricks [missiles]. And of the dozen rocket ships, I think two survived—one other and his. It was a disaster—these boats really were floating time bombs. And then, after the war, he worried about that decision, all the time. Really, a moral choice, should he have risked his ship and his men, merely to save his pride not to be late for D-Day? In point of fact, years later, he found out there was no minefield there. It had just been put on the charts to deter the Germans by his own intelligence. . . . And really, I think that experience made him an artist and made his life, and he never recovered from it.

Another story, reported by John Aldridge in *The New York Times*, illustrates the stress Golding's wartime experiences created for him:

> On one occasion a nervous tic, produced by stress and hazard, twisted his face into what appeared to be a wide grin of bloodthirsty elation. As the danger increased the grin grew even wider until, finally, his awe-struck men began whispering to one another: "Look at the Old Man. Regular fire-eater he is. The hotter it gets, the better he likes it." When the tension at last left the Golding facial muscles, the grin disappeared but was immediately replaced by an equally uncontrollable expression of acute bereavement: "Look at the Old Man now," said his men, "See how he hates it when we get out of danger. Regular fire-eater he is."

However, a person closer to him, his daughter, Judy Carver, believes that the postwar revelations of Nazi atrocities were an even more powerful influence. In an interview for the BBC documentary *Great Writers of the 20th Century: William Golding*, she says, "Towards the end of the war when they found out about the final solution [the Nazi program to exterminate the Jews] and what had been happening in the concentration camps and what people actually managed to do and the atomic bomb and he knew people who had worked on the bomb. This left him with a great feeling that systems couldn't be trusted and ideas couldn't be trusted."

Writer McCarron agrees that it was the revelation of Nazi atrocities that changed Golding's view of human nature. He says, "In one sense you could argue that really the Second World War strikes Golding retrospectively. He hadn't believed that human beings could be capable of such demonic cruelty. And the revelation that people could behave this way, I would argue, changed his life."

What shocked Golding to the core was that cultured and educated men—lawyers and doctors—could participate in Nazi atrocities and that scientists—some known to him—could build the atomic bomb.

His core beliefs would change. He began to realize that evil had nothing to do with ideology but was rooted in human nature. As Golding would say in an interview with Jack Biles,

> All this has nothing to do, directly, with Nazis or anything; it has much more to do with *people*. One had one's nose rubbed in the human condition. . . .
>
> So I saw that it was no good saying, "Well, fine. America, Britain, France, China have all won. Against the dirty swine. Because I just didn't believe it. I saw that humanity had been fighting against itself in a kind of endless war. But what had been fighting and what had been doing all these things? On the whole, *only* on the whole—I wouldn't like this to be misunderstood, as I'm *sure* it would be—if you could take the people out of the concentration camps and make concentration-camp guards of them, the situation would not be altered materially.

With this new, pessimistic world view honed by his war experiences, Golding wrote *Lord of the Flies*, "which was things I had come to believe during the war." At last, he had found his own voice and a message he passionately affirmed. This masterpiece of twentieth-century English literature examines the absolute violence and evil in human nature. Attacking British complacency, in *Lord of the Flies*, Golding says that violence and evil can happen anywhere, because humanity is innately evil.

In the essays that follow, critics explore the theme of violence in Golding's first published novel, *Lord of the Flies*.

Chronology

1911

William Golding is born in Cornwall, England, to Alec and Mildred Golding on September 19.

1930

Golding enters Brasenose College, Oxford, to study science and then switches to literature.

1934

Golding's first work, *Poems*, is published.

1935

Golding graduates from Oxford with a bachelor of arts degree.

1935–1939

Golding acts at Hampstead Everyman Theatre and Citizen House in Bath and then at a small off–West End London theater.

1939

Golding and Ann Brookfield are married; he begins teaching English and philosophy at Bishop Wordsworth's School in Salisbury.

1940–1945

Golding enlists in the Royal Navy and serves on various ships throughout World War II.

1945

Golding returns to teaching at Bishop Wordsworth's School.

1954

Lord of the Flies is published.

1955

The Inheritors is published; Golding becomes a Fellow of the Royal Society of Literature.

1956

Pincher Martin is published.

1958

The Brass Butterfly is first performed at Oxford.

1959

Free Fall is published.

1960

Golding receives a master of arts degree from Oxford and leaves teaching to devote himself to writing full-time.

1960–1962

Golding is a book reviewer for *The Spectator*.

1961–1962

Golding is writer-in-residence at Hollins College, Virginia, and does an American college lecture tour.

1964

The Spire is published.

1965

The Hot Gates and Other Occasional Pieces is published.

1966

Golding becomes an Honorary Fellow of Brasenose College, Oxford.

1967

The Pyramid is published.

1970

Golding receives an honorary doctor of letters from Sussex University.

1971

The Scorpion God is published.

1979

Darkness Visible is published.

1980

Rites of Passage is awarded the Booker-McConnell Prize for best novel of 1980.

1982

A Moving Target is published.

1983

Golding wins the Nobel Prize for Literature.

1984

The Paper Men is published.

1985

An Egyptian Journal is published.

1987

Golding publishes *Close Quarters*.

1988

Golding is knighted by Queen Elizabeth II.

1989

Golding publishes *Fire Down Below*.

1991

Golding publishes *To the Ends of the Earth*.

1993

Golding dies in Cornwall, England, on June 19.

1995

The Double Tongue is published posthumously.

CHAPTER 1

Social Issues
in Literature

Background on
William Golding

The Life of William Golding

Michael C. Prusse

Michael C. Prusse is a professor at the Pädagogische Hochschule Zürich (Zurich University of Teacher Education) in Switzerland.

In the following excerpt from his biographical and critical essay on William Golding, Michael C. Prusse traces the chronology of Golding's life and his relatively late blooming as a major twentieth-century British author. Golding was in his early forties when his first novel, Lord of the Flies, *was published. Prusse suggests that Golding's experiences during World War II deeply influenced him and helped to shape his early novels. In particular, his theme that the capacity for both good and evil resides within humankind has its roots in Golding's wartime experiences.* Lord of the Flies *is both a gripping adventure story and a fable depicting the evil that is inherent in the boys and dooms their efforts to create a civilization on the island.*

The novels of William Golding can be characterized as depicting individuals or isolated groups of human beings in archetypal circumstances, confronted with their humanity and experiencing the limits of civilization. By focusing on man's capacity for both good and evil, Golding's fiction frequently displays the quality of fable or approximates myth—the latter is the taxonomy [classification] that the novelist himself preferred. . . .

D-Day's Effect on Golding

William Gerald Golding was born in St. Columb Minor (near Newquay) in Cornwall on 19 September 1911. His father, Alec Golding, was a schoolteacher, while his mother, Mildred (née

Michael C. Prusse, "William Golding," *Dictionary of Literary Biography, vol. 330, Nobel Prize Laureates in Literature, Part 2,* Farmington Hills, MI: Gale, 2007, pp. 164–83. Copyright © 2007 Gale, a part of Cengage Learning. Reproduced by permission of Gale, a part of Cengage Learning.

Curnoe), was a keen supporter of the suffragettes [a group advocating women's right to vote]. Golding had one older brother, Jose, and a younger adopted sister, Eileen (actually his first cousin). Golding's father taught at Marlborough Grammar School in Wiltshire, and like his older brother, Golding went to school there before going on to Brasenose College Oxford in 1930, where he studied natural sciences for two years. Feeling dissatisfied with his subject, he opted for English literature instead and graduated in 1935. During his time at Oxford the future novelist published his first book, a slim volume of poems. Before and after studying for a Diploma in Education he held a series of odd jobs as a teacher, part-time actor, stage manager, and producer. On 30 September 1939, just after the outbreak of World War II, he married Ann Brookfield and became a teacher at Bishop Wordsworth's School in Salisbury.

Golding joined the Royal Navy in December 1940 and served on various ships until the end of the war, except for some time in New York and a period spent on a weapons-development program. He was involved in the pursuit of the *Bismarck* [giant Nazi warship ordered sunk by the British government] and was deeply affected by the deaths and injuries he witnessed. His service on minesweepers, destroyers, cruisers, and a rocket launcher—which he commanded at the rank of lieutenant—left a lasting impression on Golding and acutely influenced his early novels. According to Golding's friend the British historian and writer Andrew Sinclair (in a 1996 BBC documentary on Golding), the writer's decision to take his rocket ship—a "flying timebomb"—across a minefield in order to be in time for the D-Day operations had a profound effect since Golding had to weigh the moral choice of risking the lives of his men against being late for the assault on the beaches of Normandy. Later, he discovered that the minefield did not exist—it had been put on the map to deter the Germans—and this incident provided the author with an example of how questions about life and death can be conjured up and lead to passionate involvement when, in reality, there is no foundation for them.

Lord of the Flies Rejected Twenty-One Times

After the war, Golding returned to teaching English, philosophy, and the classics in Salisbury and wrote several novels. Publishers rejected all of them, and even his best-known book, *Lord of the Flies* (1954), collected twenty-one rejection slips until publisher Charles Monteith picked the manuscript up from a pile of rejects and noticed the comment of the professional reader. As Monteith recalled in "Strangers from Within", the reader's verdict began with the words "Absurd and uninteresting fantasy" and ended with "Rubbish and dull. Pointless." Nevertheless, Monteith read the manuscript and was intrigued by it, a fascination that led to the subsequent publication of the novel by Faber and Faber in 1954.

Lord of the Flies—the title is a literal translation of *Beelzebub* [Satan] from Hebrew—is an allegorical dystopia [an imaginary place where conditions are bad, the opposite of utopia] that relates the fate of a group of schoolboys who are evacuated during a future nuclear war and whose plane crashes on a desert island in the tropics. Since there are no adult survivors, the boys at first attempt to act sensibly to ensure their survival: "We've got to have rules and obey them. After all, we're not savages. We're English; and the English are best at everything. So we've got to do the right things." Ralph is elected as their leader, whereas Jack, "chapter chorister and head boy," becomes his chief rival. Jack's choirboys turn into hunters who chase and kill the feral pigs on the island, while Ralph's chief supporters—Piggy, a fat, bespectacled intellectual, and Simon, who suffers from epilepsy and later becomes a Cassandra-like [after the Greek mythological figure] prophet figure—build shelters.

The first dispute results from the signal fire that the group keeps going on the mountain and which the hunters fail to sustain because they are all involved in chasing a pig, and thus a ship passing by fails to rescue them. Furthermore, the boys are frightened by "the beast"—a product of their imagination that seems to become real when they mistake a dead parachutist hanging between the trees for physical evidence of the beast. When Simon rushes out of the jungle to inform them that the beast is in fact just a corpse, the panicked boys assume he is the beast and kill him. Simon is the only one to be illuminated about the residence of evil within themselves when the "Lord of the Flies"—in fact a pig's skull on a stake beset by flies—tells him that he is not a beast that can be hunted and killed: "I'm part of you." Though he perceives that the true beast resides within the boys themselves, he cannot communicate this insight.

When Jack loses another leadership contest against Ralph, there is a rift between them that results in the former founding a tribal society. Gradually all the boys drift into Jack's camp, and when Ralph leads his last three supporters to negotiate, Piggy is killed and the others are taken prisoner. Ralph is chased like a pig across the island and eventually, in despair, stumbles onto the beach, where he encounters a British officer and is saved. The basic idea of this novel is, according to [critics] Carmen Callil and Colm Tóibín, "that within us all, eagerly waiting to be let out, lie savages."

In his essay "Fable," Golding confirms what the words of the officer ("Jolly good show. Like the Coral Island") already spelled out: that he consciously rewrote Robert Ballantyne's Victorian adventure novel *The Coral Island* with a view to challenge its simplistic message of English supremacy. Golding even kept the names of two of Ballantyne's main characters, Ralph and Jack. Instead of the third one, Peterkin, Golding uses an almost biblical figure, Simon, who, like the man from Cyrene, is "compelled to bear his cross" (Matthew 27:32). The novelist also compares the boys' urge to conquer the island to British imperial sway, encouraging critics such as Kevin Mc-Carron to maintain that Golding was writing about colonialism in the tradition of Rudyard Kipling, George Orwell, Winifred Holtby, Joyce Cary, and Paul Scott. William Shakespeare's *The Tempest* might be added to the list since it also deals with the subduing and domination of wild and aboriginal forces in the figure of Caliban.

The main theme of Golding's fiction—the truth about human nature, the capacity for both good and evil—permeates his first novel. In "Fable" he documents the various thoughts that led to the conception of the narrative. He freely admits that *Lord of the Flies* is an adventure story that carries a moral message: the purpose of the adventure is to serve as sugar coating, which is necessary to entice readers into learning their moral lesson. The novelist was moved by his experiences of World War II to think that mankind was incorrigible in its habits: "man produces evil as a bee produces honey." He was struck by Ballantyne's notion in *The Coral Island* that evil resides outside its three protagonists and is present only in the savages and pirates that visit the islands. *Lord of the Flies*, according to Golding, describes the boys' attempt at constructing a civilization on the island, which "breaks down in blood and terror because the boys are suffering from the terrible disease of being human." Apart from the movie versions—Peter Brook filmed the first version in 1963, and another debuted in 1990—there exists one dramatized version that Golding approved of, by the British novelist and playwright Nigel Williams (first performed by students in 1991 and professionally in 1995).

In this productive phase of his life, which kept Golding writing in addition to his teaching duties, he published two more novels, *The Inheritors* in 1955 and *Pincher Martin* [in] 1956. *The Inheritors* relates the fate of a small group of Neanderthals who struggle for survival in the harsh environmental circumstances of the Stone Age and of their lethal encounter with the ancestors of mankind, *Homo sapiens.* . . .

Golding Builds His Reputation

Many critics claim that *The Inheritors* is Golding's greatest achievement. The writer Arthur Koestler called it "an earthquake in the petrified forest of the English novel." Monteith believed it to be "the best book he ever wrote" and asserted (in the BBC documentary) that Golding himself thought so too. . . .

Golding's third novel, *Pincher Martin,* concentrates on one individual, namely Christopher Hadley Martin, who saves himself from a destroyer that was torpedoed by a German submarine by swimming to a rock in the middle of the Atlantic. On this rock Martin, by means of flashbacks, is confronted with his rather unpleasant personality: "I am who I was." One particularly shocking memory evokes the coldness with which Martin raped his best friend's fiancée. His nickname, Pincher, refers both to the greed that makes him such an unattractive person and to the intense tenacity with which he clings to life. The protagonist attempts to create his reality—his life—by creating this rock in the middle of the Atlantic, by naming its different parts and by continuously asserting his belief that rescue is imminent. The novel refers to certain philosophical positions assumed by Jean-Paul Sartre and Albert Camus, the two leading French exponents of existentialism, and also directly alludes to myth when Martin declares: "I am Atlas [Greek mythological Titan who supported the heavens]. I am Prometheus [Greek mythological Titan who stole fire from Zeus and gave it to mortals]." Martin is clearly a Sisyphus [mythological king who was punished by having to roll a rock up a hill, only to watch it roll down, and to repeat this forever] figure, indebted to Camus and his essay *The Myth of Sisyphus* [translated into English in 1955]. Like the French existentialists, Golding is concerned with the question of choice:

"You gave me the power to choose and all my life you led me carefully to this suffering because the choice was my own." Eventually, Martin's tale of endurance on the rock is exposed as no more than the hallucinations of a drowning man, a mirage that echoes the miraculous but illusory escape of the protagonist who is hanged in Ambrose Bierce's "An Occurrence at Owl Creek Bridge" (1892). . . .

Golding's growing reputation drew him into the London literary scene and permitted him to supplement his income by writing essays, reviews, and travel reports. In 1955 he was made a fellow of the Royal Society of Literature. Golding's novella "Envoy Extraordinary" was published in a collective volume of three narratives in 1956; the other contributions were by John Wyndham and Mervyn Peake. Two years later, in 1958, he transformed this story into a play, *The Brass Butterfly*, which was first performed in Oxford and toured the provinces before appearing in London. In the following year he published his fourth novel, *Free Fall* (1959), as well as many reviews and travel pieces.

Free Fall is the quest into the past of the artist Sammy Mountjoy, who wants to find "the point where I began," to discover at what point in his life he lost his "innocence" and chose to become "evil." Looking back at his childhood, he describes himself as "wandering in paradise. I can only guess our innocence, not experience it." Apart from the obvious allusion to [William] Blake's *Songs of Innocence and Experience*, Golding refers to one of his favorite themes—namely, the notion of a fall from paradise that inevitably occurs in the course of human lives. Sammy's surname has frequently been read as a variation on the theme of paradise, but it is also the name of a well-known prison in Dublin—a metaphor that fittingly describes Sammy's condition: trapped in choices. . . .

The novel furthermore carries an autobiographical touch, illuminating Golding's wandering between the world of science and the spiritual: Nick, the science master, is based upon Golding's father, as the author admitted in an interview. . . .

The Spire, the novel that was inspired by his residence in Salisbury and the impressive town cathedral, was published in 1964. Golding wrote, in *A Moving Target* (1982), that he was prompted to write about this building because of the curious absence of it in Anthony Trollope's Barsetshire novels. In *The Spire*, set in the fourteenth century, Dean Jocelin acts on his vision that God has selected him to erect a tower rising to four hundred feet above Barchester Cathedral, and he pursues this goal ruthlessly and persistently, regardless of costs, particularly of human lives. The workmen murder a crippled employee of the cathedral, possibly as a heathen sacrifice for the impossible task, and the dean is aware of this incident and other unchristian proceedings. The builder, aptly named Roger Mason, who has an illicit relationship with the wife of the murdered man, sets his technological knowledge against Jocelin's fanatic faith: according to the builder, the foundations cannot support the weight of such a construction. Against all expectations the spire rises triumphantly, while those involved in its construction are either dead or dying. . . .

In 1965 Golding published *The Hot Gates and Other Occasional Pieces*, a collection of his essays, followed in 1967 by *The Pyramid*, a narrative with several autobiographical elements; the title alludes to Golding's lifelong fascination with Egyptology. The collection of essays also includes two autobiographical pieces, "Billy the Kid" and "The Ladder and the Tree," in which the roots of Golding's love of books are traced back to his childhood. The *Pyramid*, apart from focusing on growing up in an English country town with the telling name of Stilbourne (a village nearby is just as tellingly called Bumstead), presents a harsh analysis of the British class system. . . .

Golding, who was a keen amateur pianist, conceived a narrative that abounds with music and musical allusions. . . . The

William Golding. Paul Schutzer/Time Life Pictures/Getty Images.

sonata form of the story was, as Golding commented in an interview ..., not conceived from the beginning; but once he became aware of this slant, the novelist decided to adopt this structure: "I more precisely shaped it in that direction so that the last story about the old music teacher is really an air and variations: it comes back in different forms." The middle part is clearly a scherzo [a musical joke], and although Golding is frequently described as a novelist lacking in humor, *The Pyramid* shows traces of farce and is, on the whole, quite funny.

Despite these features, *The Pyramid* did not fare well with the critics, who diagnosed deteriorating creative faculties. The same fate met the novelist's next publication, *The Scorpion God* (1971), a volume consisting of three long stories or novellas, namely "The Scorpion God," "Clonk, Clonk," and "Envoy Extraordinary." ...

Golding Suffers from Depression

The late 1960s and the early 1970s were an arid period in Golding's writing career; apart from writer's block, he suffered from depression and struggled with alcohol. While wrestling with these difficulties he wrote two novels: *Darkness Visible* (1979), which won the James Tait Black Memorial Prize, and *Rites of Passage* (1980), which was declared winner of the Booker Prize. In the period leading up to the genesis of these narratives the novelist had terrible dreams that he noted in his diary, and out of these nightmares the hellish visions of *Darkness Visible* arose. . . .

The title, *Darkness Visible*, is an allusion to John Milton's *Paradise Lost*, specifically to the moment when Lucifer surveys his new abode and notices the horrible lightless dungeon, where, by means of "darkness visible," he perceives nothing but "sights of woe." . . .

Most critics were surprised at the comparatively light-hearted tone of *Rites of Passage*, which followed *Darkness Visible*. However, the narrative is not without its grave moments, since it relates the fate of a clergyman who shames himself in public and consequently wills himself to die. The story is told by Edmund Talbot, a young man of neoclassical tastes, who is extremely conceited and destined to become a member of the governor's entourage in New South Wales. He travels aboard an unnamed old ship of the line—her name is presumably *Britannia*—to the Antipodes [Australia] and in the course of the passage, he undergoes several rites that nudge him toward maturity. The ship features a microcosm of British society: apart from the tyrannical captain, Anderson, who tolerates Talbot because he writes a journal for his godfather, who is a rich and influential politician, the vessel carries several emigrants of various classes as well as the officers and crew.

In 1982 the author published *A Moving Target*, a collection of essays, reviews, and travel accounts. The title essay, his "Address to Les Anglicistes" at a congress in Rouen in 1976, illustrates some of Golding's notions concerning the state and the future of the novel. In an obvious admonition to this audience of academics and professional critics, the author censures the tendency of critics to entomb living writers in theoretical pigeonholes, which do not account for the writer's potential for development. . . .

Nobel Prize in Literature

In 1983 Golding was awarded the Nobel Prize in Literature, an announcement that caused some controversy. The London newspapers of 7 October 1983 carried headlines such as "Row over Golding's Nobel Prize" (*Times*) or "Uproar as Golding Takes Nobel Prize" (*Daily Telegraph*). The Academy secretary, Lars Gyllensten, had originally informed reporters that the choice of Golding was the result of a smooth and almost unanimous selection process. Julian Isherwood, relying on sources from within the Nobel committee, noted in the *Daily Telegraph* that two voting sessions had been required to give Golding the award—the French author Claude Simon (who eventually won the prize in 1985) coming in a close second. In any case, Gyllensten's announcement was contested by the Swedish poet Artur Lundkvist, a fierce opponent of an award to Golding, who claimed in a *Guardian* article by Paul Keel and W. L. Webb that the second vote took place in his absence and that the decision of the committee amounted to a coup against him. Furthermore, as Michael Specter records, Lundkvist dismissed Golding as "a little English phenomenon of no special interest." A further dissenting voice belonged to *Time* critic Paul Gray, who agreed with Lundkvist that Golding "was decent but hardly in the Nobel Prize class." According to Gray, Golding "should have been spared both the Nobel Prize and the controversy surrounding its unexpected arrival."

Despite this harsh criticism, the majority of the commentators applauded the Swedish Academy's decision. In an article in *Newsweek*, Peter S. Prescott even showed surprise at the "rift in the secrecy that traditionally attends the Academy's proceedings" because he qualified Golding's selection as sensible. Fellow writers also reacted in a positive fashion: as Keel and Webb reported, Doris Lessing stated that she was "absolutely delighted" with the decision, while John Fowles, best known for his novel *The French Lieutenant's Woman*, expressed his conviction that Golding was "the best British novelist of his generation." . . .

The honor brought certain side effects with it, as Judy Carver, Golding's daughter, recalls in a 2004 essay about her parents' lives: "My father became a quarry—for journalists, zealous readers, academics," even sightseers. Golding consequently left the proximity of London in 1985 and moved to an elegant Georgian house near Truro in Cornwall. Golding, who remarked in [a] 1986 interview . . . that there "is nothing to a writer but his books," resented the intrusions into his private life, and his apparently vitriolic reaction to literary paparazzi is evident in his first post-Nobel novel, *The Paper Men*.

[Victoria] Glendinning, in [an] *Observer* article, called *The Paper Men* Golding's "tragicomic cautionary tale for all literary biographers." In fact, *The Paper Men* not only comments on certain vulture-like excesses observable in some academics when focusing on the papers of a specific author but also presents a deeply disturbing portrait of a writer. Ultimately, the novel unveils the symbiotic relationship between author and critic and, as McCarron explains, addresses the issue raised by Roland Barthes and later hotly debated in academic circles, namely, the literary theory that postulates "the death of the author." . . .

Those readers who understand *The Paper Men* simply as a determined attack on academic literary criticism are misled: the novelist was clearly aware of his public role. As he had already stated in "Fable," he no longer believed "that the author has a sort of patria potestas ["power of the father"] over his brainchildren. Once they are printed they have reached their majority and the author has no more authority over them, knows no more about them, perhaps knows less about them than the critic who comes fresh to them, and sees them not as the author hoped they would be, but as what they are."

Knighthood

In the course of his career the novelist was awarded many honorary doctorates by universities; his country also recognized his stature and, having been made a Commander of the Order of the British Empire (CBE) in 1966, Golding was knighted by the queen in 1988. The year before, he had published *Close Quarters*, a sequel to *Rites of Passage*, and in 1989 *Fire Down Below* completed the sea trilogy. Two years later, in a rare case of editing his work, Golding revised the three books and Faber and Faber released them in a single volume titled *To the Ends of the Earth*. In his foreword to the trilogy Golding admits that he "did not foresee volumes two and three" when he wrote *Rites of Passage.* . . .

When Golding died in his Cornwall home on 19 June 1993, he was in the process of revising another completed novel, *The Double Tongue*—the title was the one that the novelist had written on the manuscript. The book, posthumously published by Faber and Faber in 1995, resumes the novelist's fascination with the Greeks. Set in Delphi in the first century B.C., it traces the careers of Arieka, the Pythia at the famous oracle of Delphi (she is the first-person narrator of events), and of her mentor, Ionides Peisistrades, the homosexual priest of Apollo. The notion of one age waning—here, the Greek— and another one ascending, namely, the Roman Empire, is one of the author's favorite topics and is once again employed to describe the human condition. Despite "its unpolished state," Medcalf writes, "*The Double Tongue* is as intransigent, as fresh as any of Golding's greatest novels."

The novelist's death was widely regretted: Glendinning, for instance, in her *Observer* article, described the author as the "Grand Old Man" of the British literary scene. She also noted that Golding "believed in a god, but rejected organised religion." The lack of an official biography—[journalist John] Carey has been commissioned to write it—makes it difficult to assess the accuracy of such statements. It appears, however, that the novelist, raised as an atheist and set for a career as a scientist, was brought to a halt by some sort of spiritual crisis, and, as Medcalf writes, "Golding's sense of his own creativity was deeply bound up with his belief in God."

In an interview included in the 1996 BBC documentary, William Golding declared that he was first and foremost a storyteller: "What matters to me is that there should be a story with a beginning, a middle, and an end." This approach is too modest for an author who could be characterized in the words that Talbot uses for Prettiman in *Fire Down Below*: "his mind ranged vastly through the universe of space and time as it did through the other universe of books!"

Golding Took Many Years to Find His Voice

William Golding, Interviewed by Jack Biles

Jack Biles is a literary critic who has written several books and essays on authors, including British Novelists Since 1900. *He was also an interviewer for the BBC program* Monitor.

There are two kinds of authors, Jack Biles writes in the following interview and essay: authors like Louisa May Alcott, who write about the world they know, and authors like William Golding, who let their imagination loose to write about things they have never experienced. Golding says in his interview with Biles that he wrote unsuccessfully for many years until he found his own voice. He also credits ancient Greek literature with having a profound influence on his writing.

Because Golding was forty-three when *Lord of the Flies* was published, a BBC "Monitor" interviewer observed in 1959, "This seems rather late to start writing." Golding responded, "I didn't start writing when I was forty; I had been writing ever since I was seven. I suppose you can say I've been effectively writing since I was thirty-five. I published my first book, or had my first book published, a book of verse, when I was nineteen [actually, when he was twenty-three—published October 30, 1934]. I'll say very little more about that; I just want to forget that one. Nobody knows anything about it. And then, out of the rest, you've got to take five years for the war, in the navy, and ten years, perhaps, learning to write by imitating other people and learning very late that, of course, I was merely writing other people's novels instead of my own. And it was not until I was thirty-seven, I suppose, that I grasped the great truth that you've got to write your own books and nobody else's. Then everything followed from that."

Biles: Do you remember the professor in one of Louisa May Alcott's books—Little Women, I guess—advising Jo to quit writing foolish romances about kings and castles and other things that she did not know about? He said for her to go home and write about what she did know about. It sounds somewhat like Sir Philip Sidney. Good advice, wouldn't you say?

Golding: I don't know. I think it depends somewhat upon the person, doesn't it? I don't think it is altogether good advice.

How do you mean?

Some of the fun of writing is writing what you didn't think you could. This is a curious kind of thing, a book which is impossible, anyway. After all, I have never been drowned, and I have never been flung up on a rock—never been to hell, in so many words. And therefore this is anti–Louisa May Alcott stuff I'm talking.

I see.

Writing is not reportage, but imagination. Therefore, I don't think you ever write about what you know about. You write about what you guess about and what you imagine about. This is one way of doing it.

You can be Anthony Trollope and write about things you do know about, but that is another kind of writing. Or you can be Louisa May Alcott. She knew about this New England Providence, this sort of family, this sort of house, and all the rest of it; so she chose to write that way, and that is why she made her professor say what he did. But if I had had the handling of that professor, I would have made him say, "Look, my dear girl, the trouble with you is, you are writing the book that you *ought* to write—these fantastic adventures—but you just can't do it. So, what had you best do? Just get back to the tiny little book you *can* write."

I still don't think that you really are disagreeing, in a special sense. Here we are back to semantics again. Perhaps it is not so much what you know about as it is what you care about, what you are concerned with. I grant you haven't been drowned and I grant you haven't been literally in hell, but you have been in the navy, you have seen men who were drowned, you are concerned about hell, you have thought about it, so that, perhaps, we are really arguing about "know about" and "intellectually concerned with."

Yes. It's not a straight A or B, is it?. . .

I know you have been over this fifty times, but I'd like to be clear. I have made the point several times that people had better pay attention to what you say about the sources of your books, because you have said many times that they have relatively little genesis outside yourself. And you freely acknowledge and point to them, like The Coral Island *and* Lord of the Flies. *James R. Baker in his book makes a great deal of Greek literature. I can see this, of course; for example, the Prometheus business in* Pincher Martin, *and so on. There is a strong element, certainly. Would you say that the principal literary influence upon you is Greek drama, history, mythology, and so on? Do you think that is the major influence on you?*

You are talking about literature?

Yes.

It ought to be. I would think the Aristotelian concept of tragedy is probably something that I have taken without really wondering in the Brechtian sense whether I should take it. In fact, I have been wondering more and more, lately, whether perhaps I haven't been too much concerned with the tragic hero and whether this isn't one of the reasons why my books lack a number of dimensions of reality. *Because* this is a highly specialized, highly stylized, very laudable, and youthful view of what a performance should be, what a dramatic act or an act of art, if you like, should be. But we don't really, any longer, make statues the way the Greeks made; so why should we take

Aristotle's word for tragedy when we've got other—I'm talking now as a maker, you see. This is not a question of feeling or anything else, it is a question of technique. You want to do so and so; well, obviously, you have to have a tragic hero, who starts with a flaw and ends up at the bottom. I think I took that for granted, I just accepted that, perhaps less out of Aristotle than out of Greek tragedy itself, which is in a way a bond to Aristotle, isn't it? I think it is true that Greek literature really has been the *big* literary influence in my life, but I think that that may very well have come to an end, and so may I.

Golding's Novels Are Serious in Theme and Exciting in Plot

Lars Gyllensten

Lars Gyllensten was an author, a physician, and a member of the Swedish Academy.

In the following speech, made when presenting William Golding the 1983 Nobel Prize in Literature, Lars Gyllensten compares him to American novelist Herman Melville. The works of both authors share compelling story lines along with profound depths of meaning. World War II dramatically changed Golding's beliefs, Gyllensten contends. Golding no longer believed in the ability of humanity to improve society—rather, he believed that the problems in society had their roots in the evil present in human nature. Gyllensten maintains that his vision is saved from pessimism, however, by a religious element: along with evil, humanity also possesses a belief in God. The tension between these warring impulses forms the theme for many of Golding's works, Gyllensten notes.

William Golding's first novel—*Lord of the Flies*, 1954— rapidly became a world success and has so remained. It has reached readers who can be numbered in tens of millions. In other words, the book was a bestseller, in a way that is usually granted only to adventure stories, light reading and children's books. The same goes for several of his later novels.

Entertaining Yet Complex

The reason is simple. These books are very entertaining and exciting. They can be read with pleasure and profit without the need to make much effort with learning or acumen [accu-

Lars Gyllensten, "Presentation Speech: The Nobel Prize in Literature 1983," *Nobel Lectures, Literature 1981–1990*, edited by Tore Frangsmyr and Sture Allen, Hackensack, NJ: World Scientific Publishing Co., 1993. Copyright © The Nobel Foundation 1983. Reproduced by permission.

racy of insight]. But they have also aroused an unusually great interest in scholars, writers and other interpreters, who have sought and found deep strata of ambiguity and complication in Golding's work. In those who use the tools of narration and linguistic art they have incited to thinking, discovery and creation of their own, in order to explore the world we live in and to settle down in it. In this respect William Golding can perhaps be compared to the American Herman Melville, whose works are full of equivocal profundity as well as fascinating adventure. In fact the resemblance extends farther than that. Golding has a very keen sight and sharp pen when it comes to the power of evil and baseness in human beings. He often chooses his themes and the framework for his stories from the world of the sea or from other challenging situations in which odd people are tempted to reach beyond their limits, thereby being bared to the very marrow. His stories usually have a fairly schematic drama, almost an anecdote, as skeleton. He then covers this with a richly varied and spicy flesh of colourful characters and surprising events.

It is the pattern of myth that we find in his manner of writing.

Effect of World War II

A very few basic experiences and basic conflicts of a deeply general nature underlie all his work as motive power. In one of his essays he describes how as a young man he took an optimistic view of existence. He believed that man would be able to perfect himself by improving society and eventually doing away with all social evil. His optimism was akin to that of other utopians [idealistic reformers], for instance [English writer] H.G. Wells. The Second World War changed his outlook. He discovered what one human being is really able to do to another. And it was not a question of headhunters in New Guinea or primitive tribes in the Amazon region. They were atrocities committed with cold professional skill by well-educated and cultured people—doctors, lawyers and those with a long tradition of high civilization behind them. They carried out their crimes against their own equals. He writes:

> "I must say that anyone who moved through those years without understanding that man produces evil as a bee produces honey, must have been blind or wrong in the head."

Golding inveighs [protests] against those who think that it is the political or other systems that create evil. Evil springs from the depths of man himself—it is the wickedness in human beings that creates the evil systems or that changes what from the beginning is, or could be, good into something iniquitous [wicked] and destructive.

The Myth of the Fall

There is a mighty religious dimension in William Golding's conception of the world, though hardly Christian in the ordinary sense. He seems to believe in a kind of Fall. Perhaps rather one should say that he works with the myth of a Fall. In some of his stories, chiefly the novel *The Inheritors*, 1955, we find a dream of an original state of innocence in the history of mankind. The Fall came with the motive power of a new species. The aggressive intelligence, the power-hungry self-assertion and the overweening individualism are the source of evil and violence—individual as well as social violence. But these qualities and incentives are also innate in man as a created being. They are therefore inseparably a part of his character and make themselves felt when he gives full expression to himself and forms his societies and his private destiny.

We come across this tragic drama in many different ways in William Golding's novels. In *Lord of the Flies* a group of young boys are isolated on a desert island. Soon a kind of primitive society takes shape and is split into warring factions, one marked by decency and willingness to co-operate, the

Man's conscience or a representation of the choice between good and evil that each person must make. Created by Garif Basyrov. © Images.com/Corbis.

other by worship of force, lust for power and violence. The novel *Pincher Martin*, 1956, depicts how the main character, the narrator, is drowning. In his passionate absorption in himself he seems for a time to get the better of death. He does so by recounting his life, a life full of ruthless egoism and cruelty to others, a miserable life yet it was his and on no account does he want to lose it. He, the dead man, tries to make the rock to which he is clinging into a picture of himself. It is a weird ghost story, a fable of a will to live without shame or moderation.

In the novel *Rites of Passage*, 1980, the drama is enacted in the microcosm that the author arranges on a ship of the line at the beginning of the 19th Century. The book gives a cruel and drastic description of social barriers and aggressions on this ship, with an underlying black comedy and a masterly command of the characters' various linguistic roles. The scapegoat—one of many in Golding's works—is a priest who, naively trusting in the authority of his office, tries to assert his own dignity. He is subjected to outrages, each worse than the last, himself taking part in them, and ends up in such a desperate situation that he dies of shame.

Evil Is Present, but So Is God

All is not evil in the world of mankind, however, and all is not black in William Golding's imagined world. According to him, man has two characteristics—the ability to murder is one, belief in God the other. Innocence is not entirely lost. There is a striving away from evil. This striving often goes astray in self-assertion and illusionism. But it is there nevertheless and is allied with something that is not merely human. In the novel *The Spire*, 1964, this striving is imbodied in a story about the building of a medieval cathedral. The builder is a priest who believes he has been ordered by God to build a spire that defies all reasonable calculations and measurements. His striving is both good and bad, containing the most complex reasons—humility and conviction but also arrogance, wilfulness and furtive sexual motives.

William Golding's novels and stories are not only sombre moralities and dark myths about evil and about treacherous, destructive forces. As already mentioned they are also colourful tales of adventure which can be read as such, full of narrative joy, inventiveness and excitement. In addition there are plentiful streaks of humour, biting irony, comedy and drastic jesting. There is a vitality which breaks through what is tragic and misanthropic [hateful of mankind], frightening in fact. A vitality, a vigour, which is infectious owing to its strength and intractability and to the paradoxical freedom it possesses as against what is related. His fabled world is tragic and pathetic, yet not overwhelming and depressing. There is a life which is mightier than life's conditions.

Golding Was a Major Novelist Who Took on Important Themes

The Times of London

The Times of London is a major daily newspaper in the United Kingdom.

In summing up William Golding's illustrious career at the time of his death, The Times *(London) in the following piece praises the scope of his writing with its vast spectrum of serious themes, broad field of subjects, and sweeping range of style and mood. As a man, Golding possessed an independence of spirit that caused him to remain apart from literary movements and to be a risk taker in his writings. Although there is disagreement among critics as to which is his best novel, his first,* Lord of the Flies, *is his most widely read.*

Sir William Golding, CBE [Commander of the Order of the British Empire], English novelist and winner of the Nobel Prize for Literature (1983), died suddenly at his home near Truro, Cornwall, on June 19 aged 81. He was born in St Columb Minor, Cornwall, on September 19, 1911.

William Golding was one of only four English authors (the others are [Rudyard] Kipling, [John] Galsworthy and Winston Churchill) to receive the Nobel Prize for Literature. Some felt it might justly have gone to Graham Greene, Anthony Powell or James Hanley, but none questioned his suitability for the award, as is so often the case.

Golding Created Several Major Works

He was a "big" novelist, most of whose work could usually carry the weight he put into it. He lived outside literary coteries [cliques], struggled with grave and ponderous themes, and took risks which lesser writers could not dare to take. As is the case with all such writers there is general disagreement about which is his masterpiece but no doubt as to whether he produced one. Is it *Lord of the Flies* (1954), *The Inheritors* (1955), *The Spire* (1964), *Darkness Visible* (1979) or the last trilogy consisting of *Rites of Passage, Close Quarters* and *Fire Down Below* (1981–89)? This is in any case a formidable list and some would add to it.

William Gerald Golding's father, a Quaker turned atheist, was a master at Marlbrough Grammar School where William was educated. He then went on to Brasenose College, Oxford, from which he graduated in 1935. While still at Oxford he published, as "W.G. Golding", [the] volume *Poems* (1934) with Macmillan in London, and in New York (1935). What reviews this received were indifferent, and of the book he later declared that he made "furtive efforts to conceal, destroy, or at any rate disclaim that melancholy slim volume of my extreme youth." For some years, indeed, there was no copy of it in the British Museum Reading Room. However, slim and melancholy though it may have been, some have found in it vital clues to his later struggles and achievements.

From 1935 until 1940 and again, part-time, from 1945 to 1954 Golding worked in small theatre companies in Wiltshire as writer, actor and director. Some of his impressions of this work may be gathered from his novel *The Pyramid* (1967), not one of his best books. In 1940 he joined the Royal Navy which he admired and enjoyed "because it worked." During his service he became officer in charge of a rocket ship [a ship armed with missiles] and (and as a schoolteacher) instructed naval cadets. In 1945 he returned to Bishop Wordsworth's School, Salisbury, whose staff he had joined in 1939. He remained there until 1961 when the success of *Lord of the Flies* enabled him to resign.

A Cult Favorite

This novel was the fruition of half a lifetime. Golding was 43 when he published it. Its knowledge of youth in particular and of human nature in general was immediately apparent. Yet, anthropologically, this story of boys who, isolated from adult supervision, become brutal and self-destructive is "wrong": studies have shown that boys who are actually thus isolated do not behave as Golding had them behave in *Lord of the Flies*. The force of his fable rose from its being, not based on "fact" but on what any sensitive and highly-imaginative schoolmaster might dream up while performing his duties on a wet afternoon. It was R.M. Ballantyne's charming Victorian tale, *Coral Island*, turned on its head; but its "boys" are really terrible little men as in Kipling's *Stalky & Co* which Golding rewrites with the venom its author was unable to put into it.

Read like that, *Lord of the Flies* is the story of adults (at least males) in the 20th century with its politicians and its "experts" and its wars. Yet [London publisher] Faber's reader had originally famously said of it: "Rubbish and dull. Pointless." The public disagreed and the book quickly acquired a cult reputation, especially in the United States, where it succeeded *The Catcher in the Rye* as the most popular novel for young Americans. By the mid-1960s it had been widely translated, had sold over two million copies and had been made into a successful film (the success was part of the reason why Golding could eventually give up teaching).

Wide-Ranging Subject Matter

Golding liked to change his style and mood with each book: his gear changes were never those of a "minor" writer and his fiction covered an enormous range of subject matter from prehistoric man to 19th-century sea voyagers, from Ancient Egypt to Britain during the Blitz. *The Inheritors* (1955) is one of the most remarkable tours de force in postwar fiction of any nationality. It tells of the defeat of a group of Neanderthals at the hands of homo sapiens. Some would say this is Golding's greatest novel.

His work had at all times a pronounced sense of the religious, but nowhere more so than in his next magnificent novel, *The Spire* (1964), set in Medieval England: a priest, Jocelin, tries to crown his cathedral with a four-hundred foot spire, even against the laws of gravity. He, a "flesh dog", is inspired by angels and tempted by demons at every step.

Golding always waited until he was ready, and this meant long periods of comparative silence. The 15 years from 1964 to 1979 saw only the relatively minor *The Pyramid*, a collection of three novellas called *The Scorpion God* (1971), and a book of essays, *The Hot Gates and other Occasional Pieces* (1966). During this period Golding had almost drowned his family and himself in the English Channel while pursuing his most beloved recreation, sailing. It was, he said: "A traumatic experience which stopped me doing anything for two or three years."

In other respects, however, he made good use of his time. He kept a journal, travelled widely and developed his love of music, particularly the piano. His reputation was by now intact: he had received a CBE in 1966, and throughout the 1960s and 1970s academic articles continued to pour out. As a novelist, however, he was silent but not forgotten.

A Triumphant Return

He returned triumphantly with *Darkness Visible* (1978) and dispelled any lingering doubts among his followers that he was a one, or at most two, novel writer. *Pincher Martin* (1956) had not provoked uniformly good reviews and critics continued to quarrel over the respective merits of *Lord of the Flies* and *The Spire*, and to interpret the latter in various wild ways as anything from a Christian allegory to a Freudian phallic fantasy.

Scene from the 1963 film adaptation of William Golding's Lord of the Flies. *Two Arts/ CD/The Kobal Collection/The Picture Desk, Inc.*

Darkness Visible is set in England from 1940 to the late 1970s. It has a relatively simple, thriller-like plot at its centre, but its complex characterisation (of the boy Matty, in particular), its moral seriousness and dense symbolism attracted critics who, although they could not agree about it, recognised that they had a real, and a really tragic, book on their hands. Golding was no help: he refused interviews and was himself profoundly disturbed by what he had produced.

Of the final trilogy and the separate novel, *The Papermen* (1984), perhaps the latter, a grim parable about the trials and tribulations of a writer's life, is the more powerful and satisfying. The trilogy, beginning with *Rites of Passage*, is less intense and written at a lower level of energy, although it is a profoundly interesting work by a man by no means written out. Its first half is Golding's most exuberant and humorous work, and the one which best reveals his love-hate relationship with the sea. In the work as a whole, Golding tried to express his curiosity about and sympathy with homosexuality, and to portray the nature of male sexual desire as distinct from female. It was, as always, highly unusual.

"Miss Pulkinhorn", a short story published in *Encounter* in August 1960 and adapted for radio by Golding in that year, should be mentioned as one of Golding's outstanding uncollected works.

William Golding was a private man who was careful to stay well outside the literary politics of the metropolitan world. That independence of spirit lay at the heart of his fictional achievement. But he was also genial and courteous with friends, and those who knew him spoke warmly of him.

He had been well before his sudden collapse. He leaves a widow, Ann, whom he married in 1939, and a son and a daughter.

Violence in
Lord of the Flies

Lord of the Flies Is About Mastering the Conflicts of Puberty

Jerome Martin

Jerome Martin was chairman of the English department at Fordham Preparatory School in the Bronx, New York.

In the following article, Jerome Martin encourages students to interpret Lord of the Flies *as a story about just one character—Ralph—with all the other characters representing aspects of his personality. Ralph is entering puberty, and all of the symbols in the novel tell the story of trauma involved in leaving the security of boyhood.*

Here's a wild exercise for the readers of William Golding's *Lord of the Flies*. No high school novel tempts students to read *into* a work instead of *out from* as does this. So, if you want to cure your symbol hunters, once and for all, involve them in the following exercise.

Duplicate for your students the following list of names, events, and items mentioned in the novel. Leave sufficient space next to each for the meaning of each symbol. Names: Ralph, Piggy, Johnny, Sam 'n' Eric or Samneric, Jack, The Choir (Maurice, Simon, Roger, Robert, Henry, Harold, etc.), Percival Wemys Madison, Mulberry-color-birth-mark boy, The Officer, Littluns. Events: Taking names, Standing on his head Betraying Ralph, Blowing into the conch, Hunting pigs, Being saved. Items: Piggy's glasses, Black cloaks, Candle bushes,

Jerome Martin, "Symbol Hunting Golding's *Lord of the Flies*," *The English Journal*, vol. 58, no. 3, March 1969, pp. 408–13.

Knife, Original Sin, The conch, The Island, The Creepers, Spears and logs, Pigs, Fire, Castle Rock, The dead flyer, The Lord of the flies, Butterflies, Smoke, The Sea.

Golding's Theme

To establish an atmosphere of authenticity for what you will be saying later, announce to your students that William Golding is known to use the stylistic device of having the action of the surface story take place in a short span of time or in suspended time. . . .

Next, direct the attention of the class to what Golding says is the theme of the novel: "The theme is an attempt to trace the defects of society back to the defects of human nature." If Golding is describing human nature, it is natural to ask, "When is human nature best studied?" The answer is, "Under a crisis or a trauma." Ralph is the main character, so he must be experiencing the crisis or trauma. We read that Ralph is "old enough, twelve years and a few months, to have lost the prominent tummy of childhood." If your students can discover that this is the beginning of the puberty crisis, that is good. If they can't, you can tell them.

They should then be ready for the next leap. Announce that there is only one total character in the novel, Ralph. The others are facets of his total personality. Hopefully, your students will begin writing on the duplicated sheet of items. The young mind likes to have "answers" that he can write down.

One of the main tenets of current criticism is to look at the structure of a work and to see the interrelating parts. A symbol cannot represent one thing in a certain section of a work and then be changed later to stand for something else. With this in mind, you are ready to let your students discover what happens when literary works are read *into*. The reader creates a most elaborate and complex system of symbolic meanings. What follows may be read to the students or drawn from them through questions. As the meaning of each symbol is "revealed," the students are to jot it down.

Names in *Lord of the Flies* Have Significance

Introducing the names in the *Lord* of *the Flies* is very significant. The boy experiencing puberty is Ralph who is physically mature for his twelve years and a few months: "You could see now that he might make a boxer, as far as width and heaviness of shoulders went, but there was a mildness about his mouth and eyes that proclaimed no devil." Remembering that Golding wishes to establish human nature, we see that Piggy is next introduced. His words and actions reflect man's intellect and reasoning powers. He communicates in a way of imitating adults but with grammatically poor English, representing those who have read some truths about reality but have not made these their own through insight and/or experience. It is the job of the intellect to name things and to put labels on everything. This is exactly what Ralph tells Piggy to do, "Now go back, Piggy, and take names. That's your job. So long." This labeling is done in light of tradition and the wisdom of the ages, represented by Piggy's glasses. He rubs his glasses during crises and when making decisions. Piggy has asthma and can do no work, indicating that notional and conceptual knowledge is crippled without the experiential. It is for this reason that Piggy must be killed and washed out into the vastness and openness of the sea to become truly a meaningful facet of the whole person, Ralph. Even the dead flyer is washed out into the sea, the only hope of empty men.

Before puberty a child experiences relatively little conflict with the world or within himself. When Piggy questions, "Aren't there any grownups at all?", Ralph responds by standing on his head. This act, significantly, is done a few times at the beginning of the novel only, as Ralph sees the world through his youthful eyes.

Next on the scene is little innocent Johnny who is boyhood imagination, somewhat stilted, and for the time being satisfied by putting a pink thumb in his mouth. Later in the story Johnny cries over the images of the beastie.

With the intellect and the imagination established, Golding next presents Sam and Eric. Often written as one word, "Samneric" stand for Ralph's will. More than once they are locked in a struggling embrace because Ralph cannot always determine good from evil. They have hair like tow and are chunky and vital, but they are not completely developed as yet. One of them reveals Ralph's hiding place and betrays him. Evil does betray the man.

Another important facet of the total personality to be established after intellect, imagination, and will is emotion. Coming down the beach, "marching approximately in step in two parallel lines" are the choristers. They are wearing black cloaks "from throat to ankle" denoting the subdued state of the emotions in the boy before puberty. When they are given permission to uncover, they emerge as powerful drives. This is seen when they begin to run wild to fetch wood for the fire and "their black caps of maintenance were slid over one ear like berets." Jack Merridew (Merry Andrew) depicts pride as the leader of the emotions. Maurice, next in size, "broad and grinning all the time" is joy. Roger is hate, often acting as lust, "a furtive boy whom no one knew, who kept to himself with an inner intensity of avoidance and secrecy." Everyone gets to know Roger since he later shows the others how to use their spears. It is Roger who kills Piggy. Bill, Robert, Harold, and Henry represent other emotions with an astonishing consistency of action and word.

There is one special member of this group whom Jack dislikes intensely because he is shy and "always throwing a faint." This is Simon, pure and simple love. On one of the first adventures, Ralph picks Simon to go with Jack and himself to investigate the island. Ralph remarks, "If Simon walks in the middle of us, then we could talk over his head." It is Simon who discovers at this time the candle bushes which symbolize church rituals. Jack slashes at one of them with his knife, and an aromatic scent spills over the three boys. Jack then remarks, "Green candles. . . . We can't eat them. Come on." Pride rebels here against the immaterial. If it isn't useful, it is valueless.

A little later we become aware of a boy with a mulberry-colored birthmark "warped out of the perpendicular by the fierce light of publicity, and he bored into the grass with one toe." In all his novels, Golding seems to be preoccupied with the idea of original sin. The blemished-one is Ralph's knowledge of original sin, since Piggy is very concerned about the stained boy. This boy is the first one who wants to know what Ralph is going to do about the snake-thing. With one hand on the shell, Piggy interprets what the boy with the mulberry-colored birthmark whispers, "He says the beastie came in the dark."

Another facet of Ralph's personality is Percival Wemys Madison, The Vicarage, Harcourt St. Anthony, Hants, telephone, telephone. . . . He is memory. Percival and Phil, the emotion of fear, are the two who tell the others about the beast from the sea. At the end of the novel, Percival is greatly changed:

"I'm, I'm—"

"But there was no more to come. Percival Wemys Madison sought in his head for an incantation that had faded clean away." Ralph's memory has a different hierarchy of values after the experience of puberty.

The others in the novel, not given labels, are known by the generic title of "littluns." Human nature is too complicated to be able to label all its facets.

The Conch Shell Symbolizes Order

Early in the story Ralph points out and Piggy grabs a conch which becomes the symbol of order and authority. Ralph is the only one who is supposed to blow into the shell to create

Scene from the 1963 film adaptation of William Golding's Lord of the Flies. *Two Arts/ CD/The Kobal Collection/The Picture Desk, Inc.*

a loud blast calling all facets of the personality to attention. These assemblies, resulting from the call, are times of decision. "That's why Ralph made a meeting. So we can decide what to do," echoes Piggy. At another assembly, Jack remarks, "We'll have rules! . . . Lots of rules! Then when anyone breaks 'em—" Since there is a close connection between authority and tradition, Piggy (intellect) shrieks in terror as Jack (pride) snatches the glasses from his face, "Mind out! Give 'em back! I can hardly see! You'll break the conch!", meaning that without tradition the mind is darkened, and one would have to start all over again investigating everything. Without tradition and authority, control and direction are impossible. Paradoxically, Piggy "sees" more after losing his glasses.

Later in the novel, Ralph asks Piggy what makes things break up. To this, Piggy, rubbing his glasses, replies, "I suppose it's Jack." Piggy tells Ralph that Jack hates reason (Piggy) but respects the person (Ralph), and if Ralph were to stand out of the way, Jack would hurt the next thing and that is reason.

The Crisis in *Lord of the Flies* Is Puberty

Your students are now ready to accept Golding's special stylistic feature: suspending time. Human nature is established, and the crisis is puberty. Consider that Golding is speaking of Ralph's experience as happening during one night while the boy is in a semi-dream world existence. The island would be the boy's bed. The mountain where the vision is clear would be his head, the bridge over to Castle Rock would be his neck, and the fortress of Castle Rock itself would be his body. The creepers would be his blankets.

When his father, the naval officer, enters Ralph's bedroom at the end of the novel and sees the blankets ajar and Ralph's "filthy body, matted hair, and unwiped nose," he asks Ralph, "Who's boss here?" Ralph replies loudly, "I am." That statement then becomes the most important one in the entire novel. Ralph had experienced his first nocturnal emission. The bulk of the novel expresses the conflict one must go through before the total personality can emerge, with a certain loss of innocence, but still be boss.

Throughout the story, spears, logs, and sticks are the phallic symbol, and they become Jack's preoccupation as the leader of the hunters. These hunters, the emotions, are searching for pigs, material goods. Wanting to possess and to dominate, to kill and yet to have, the hunters allow the goods to become the end. While others concern themselves about rescue, Jack and his hunters have fun hunting for pigs with their spears. Jack dismisses the thought of a snake-thing because pride could merely destroy it. "There isn't a snake-thing. But if there was a snake we'd hunt it and kill it. We're going to hunt pigs to get meat for everybody. And we'll look for the snake too."

It is fitting that Sam and Eric are the first to find a large log which can be used for the fire. Fire throughout the novel represents the drives of man toward good and evil. "The twins, Sam 'n Eric, were the first to get a likely log but they could do nothing till Ralph, Jack, Simon, Roger, and Maurice found room for a hand-hold. Then they inched the grotesque dead thing up the rock and toppled it over on top." Golding has chosen carefully the names of those who help in this experience: Samneric (good and evil), Ralph (the person), Jack (pride), Simon (love), Roger (lust), and Maurice (joy). The author concluded this paragraph: "Once more, amid the breeze, the shouting, the slanting sunlight on the high mountain, was shed that glamour, that strange invisible light of friendship, adventure, and content."

When Jack breaks away from Ralph, Piggy, Samneric, and Simon, he and the passions find security in Castle Rock. It is from this strong fort that Jack runs his activities and seeks the pleasure of pursuit for apparent goods. There was sufficient fruit on the island to satisfy all, but this wasn't enough for Jack. He continues the destructive hunt. Even Ralph is tempted to give up the idea of rescue and go hunting, but Piggy keeps reminding him about salvation.

Simon and Piggy Are Sacrificed

Simon, who remains faithful to Ralph, plays a very important part in the novel. It is he who feeds the "littluns" the choicest fruit which they cannot reach. And after the children have followed him and have had their fill, Simon suffers the arrow of the sun until the sweat runs from his pores. He goes down on his knees three times in saving decaying man from his entanglements to tell the truth (of the dead flyer who has fallen from the sky) to the others. But Simon is killed by those whom he wished to save, and he too is washed out into the openness of the sea. Whereas Simon is sacrificed for the group (society), Piggy is sacrificed to make Ralph whole. Of course, then we ask if the following passage is not the symbol of the resurrection of the body: "Somewhere over the darkened curve of the world the sun and moon were pulling, and the film of water on the earth planet was held, bulging slightly on one side while the solid core turned. The great wave of the tide moved farther along the island and the water lifted. Softly, surrounded by a fringe of inquisitive bright creatures, itself a silver shape beneath the steadfast constellation, Simon's dead body moved out toward the open sea."

Before he is killed, however, Simon has his bout with the devil, the lord of the flies, the one who would like to lie about what Ralph is experiencing in puberty. Through his deceit, Beelzebub (god of insects) tries to take control. He does not want Ralph to be master of himself. Simon knows what it could be, but it is the devil who colors all red, not green. In this light, the statement, "Passions beat about Simon on the mountaintop with awful wings," makes sense. Butterflies (the symbol of beauty; in Greek: life, spirit, and breath) have frequently been present when Simon has communicated with nature, but they desert the place where the head of the pig is forced onto the stick sharpened at both ends. One end is jammed into a crack of *mother earth*; the other holds the head of the lord of lies. The mouth of the beast is dark, a blackness that Simon experiences spreading. The heart of darkness wants no part of love or true meaning. So the Lord of the Flies says, "I'm warning you. I'm going to get angry. D'you see? You're not wanted. Understand? We are going to have fun on this island! So don't try it on, my poor misguided boy, or else——." The way that the devil is to get ultimate control is through man's total pursuit of pleasure through materialism. Jack tries to make Simon eat of the meat of materialism, but Simon gives of his portion to Piggy, helping him experience both good and the sharing of things. "Simon, sitting between the twins and Piggy, wiped his mouth and shoved his piece of meat over the rocks to Piggy, who grabbed it. The twins giggled and Simon lowered his face in shame." Also, when Piggy loses his glasses, Simon finds them. Thus does love try to help reason.

Several other symbols have been well worked into the story. When the boys are investigating the "beast" on the mountain, they see a creature which moves as the wind blows it—the dead, hollow, decaying flyer. It is fallen man in a state of helplessness, moving as if alive. This figure has to be cleansed and washed by the rains of baptism before moving out to the sea.

Another symbol is Ralph's "shutter coming down," a flickering in his brain when he momentarily wonders about going with the others to hunt with spears. Should he go with the others to have fun, or should he be concerned about being saved? The symbol of salvation is smoke.

Ralph Loses the Security of Boyhood

As the novel progresses, the forces divide, and decisions are to be made. Simon tells Ralph that things will be all right no matter what Ralph has to go through. Simon says, "You'll get back to where you came from." Ralph is discovering himself and asks Simon, "How do you know?" Simon replies, "I just think you'll get back all right."

Towards the end of the story, Ralph is hunted by all the forces which Jack controls. In his escape from the hunters, Ralph comes upon the skull of the pig which is mounted on the stick. He knocks off the head and wrenches the stick from the earth. "Ralph drew his feet up and crouched. The stake was in his hands, the stake sharpened at both ends, the stake that vibrated so wildly, that grew long, short, light, heavy, light again."

Piggy had been killed, and the conch smashed into a thousand pieces. Samneric had been tied up and then made to join the tribe. Bill (hope) is changed, Robert (desire) is satisfied with meat, and Ralph himself is hungry. Sam gives Ralph some meat. "If there were light—" remarks Ralph.

Roger is carrying death in his hands, so Ralph tries to think. He had never gone against reason (Piggy); made fun of, yes, but never violated. And yet, "he was beginning to dread the curtain that might waver in his brain, blacking out the sense of danger making a simpleton of him."

Finally, Ralph experiences what he doesn't totally understand or want. The security of boyhood is gone, and he tries to cry for mercy while warding off what comes. Through the entire semi-dreamworld state, Ralph has experienced his first nocturnal emission. He is no longer a boy. His experience has been one of awesome mystery. He now sees the power of the passions of man and realizes how all drives must be directed if one is to emerge as a full personality.

Lord of the Flies Is About the Male Tendency to Violence

Paula Alida Roy

Paula Alida Roy is a writer and consultant who teaches at Mohawk Valley Community College and supervises student teachers at Utica College in New York. For twenty years she chaired the department of English at Westfield High School in New Jersey.

In the following essay, Paula Alida Roy argues that Golding uses the absence of any females on the island in Lord of the Flies *to demonstrate the danger of men being left alone to descend into violence. The sow is the only female on the island, and she is sodomized and slaughtered. The boy Piggy, who is described in feminine terms, is ineffective in preventing violence and then is killed himself. Roy contends that Golding is a misogynist who believes women are incapable of controlling the male impulse toward violence.*

William Golding's *Lord of the Flies* is peopled entirely by boys and, briefly, adult men. The absence of girls and women, however, does not prohibit interrogating this text for evidence of sexism/gender bias. We might begin by questioning the implicit assumptions about male violence and competitiveness that permeate Golding's Hobbesian [after British philosopher Thomas Hobbes] vision. Today's sociobiologists will embrace these boys, whose aggressive reversion to savagery "proves" the power of testosterone-fueled behavior. In fact, one approach to studying this novel could involve research into the rash of books and articles about male violence, about raising and educating boys. Teachers might ask if or how this story would be different if girls had been on the island. . . . More interesting, however, is the text itself, in which the very absence of girls or women underscores how *feminine* or *female* stands in sharp contrast to *masculine* or *male* in Golding's island world.

Ralph and Jack as Traditional Males

The three major characters, Ralph, Jack, and Piggy, form a sort of continuum of attitudes toward life as it develops on the island in relation to their past memories of "civilized" British boarding school. Ralph and Jack are both masculine boys, handsome, fit, strong. Piggy, on the other hand, is fat, asthmatic, and physically weak. Jack, the choir leader, enters equipped with a gang; the development of this group from choirboys to hunters and Jack's deterioration from strong leader to cruel tyrant offer opportunities to look at male bonding and group violence, especially when we examine rape imagery in the language of the sow-killing scene. Ralph enters the book first, alone, and develops as the individualist who struggles to maintain some sort of order amid the growing chaos.

Piggy is the pivotal character: Not only do his glasses ignite sparks for the signal fire, but it is also he who defines the role of the conch in calling assemblies and he who insists on reminding the other boys over and over again of the world of manners and civility back home. Of the three boys, in fact of all the boys, only Piggy makes constant reference to a maternal figure—his "auntie," the woman raising him. We hear no reference to Jack's mother and we learn that Ralph's mother went away when he was very young. Some of the littl'uns cry at night for their mothers, but in general, only Piggy makes repeated and specific reference to a mother figure as an influence on him.

Piggy Is Described in Female Terms

As Golding sets up the influence of Piggy's "auntie," we see that it is a mixed message about women. On the one hand, Piggy offers important reminders of civilized behavior and serves as a strong influence on and later the only support of Ralph in his efforts to keep order. On the other hand, Piggy's weakness and whining seem to be the result of the feminizing influence of his "auntie." He is, in fact, a somewhat feminized figure himself, in the negative stereotypical sense of physical softness, fearfulness, nagging. The early homoerotic connection between Ralph and Jack is underscored by Jack's jealousy of Piggy, his sarcastic derision of Ralph's concern for the weaker boy. Piggy's nickname, in fact, links him to the doomed pigs on the island, most notably the sow killed in a parody of rape by the hunters "wedded to her in lust," who "collapsed under them and they were heavy and fulfilled upon her." The identification of Piggy with the slaughtered pigs is made explicit in Piggy's death scene: "Piggy's arms and legs twitched a bit, like a pig's after it has been killed." If Piggy and the sow are the only female or feminized creatures on the island, then we can see that the one is useful only for meat and as a totemic figure and the other, the fat asthmatic boy, serves as scapegoat, victim first of ridicule, then physical abuse, and finally murder at the hands of the now savage boys under Jack's command. To the extent that he chooses to remain with Piggy, to hang on to elements of civilization, Ralph too becomes a hunted victim, "rescued" only by the appearance of the naval officer, Golding's ironic personification of adult male violence dressed up in a formal officer's uniform.

Misogyny Evident in *Lord of the Flies*

Searching the text itself, we find the female pronoun applied only to Piggy's auntie and to the sow. There are very few references to mothers, none to other women such as sisters or grandmothers. There is only one specific and direct mention of girls, quite late in the novel, when Ralph and Piggy and Sam and Eric seek to clean themselves up in preparation for a visit to Jack's camp where they plan to make a reasonable attempt to help Piggy recover his stolen glasses. Piggy insists on carrying the conch with them, and Ralph wants them to bathe: "We'll be like we were. We'll wash." When he suggests they comb their hair "only it's too long," Piggy says, "we could find some stuff . . . and tie your hair back." Eric replies, "Like a girl!" That single reference stands, along with the references to Piggy's auntie and the contrast set up by the absence of all other female figures, to identify the female with "civilization," ineffectual, far away, and dangerously weak. To return to the details of the rape-murder of the great sow, it is important to note that the sow is a mother figure, "sunk in deep maternal bliss," nursing her litter of piglets. The rape/murder of the sow and the final murder of Piggy suggest that the final movement into savagery involves the killing and defiling of the maternal female. Golding would not be the first to identify the female with attempts to control or tame male violence; he concludes that the female is unsuccessful because she is too weak, flawed, flesh-bound to overcome the ingenuity, craftiness, and sheer brutality of male violence.

Golding's Hobbesian view of human nature carries with it a whiff of misogyny [hatred of women] or at least a suspicion that what women represent has little impact, finally, on culture or civilization. The island is a boys' club shaped by the theme of "boys will be boys" when left to their own devices. Obviously allegorical, the novel invites the reader to consider the absence of girls as a symbolic presence and the perils of ultramasculinity.

Law and Order Can Control Humanity's Evil Nature

Kathleen Woodward

Kathleen Woodward is professor of English and director of the Simpson Center for the Humanities at the University of Washington. She is the author of numerous books, including Aging and Its Discontents: Freud and Other Fiction.

In the following essay Kathleen Woodward contends that in Lord of the Flies *William Golding is presenting humanity as inherently evil and implying that the atrocities that occurred in Nazi Germany could have just as easily occurred in England. It is only by avoiding complacency that man can hope to conquer the evil in his nature. Given a choice between their better impulses (represented by democracy) and their instinctive nature (represented by aggression), the boys choose the latter.*

The cheery morality of the popular children's adventure story requires at the very least a skeptical if not a cynical gaze. This is one of the points of departure of William Golding's meticulously crafted first book, *Lord of the Flies*, which was published in 1954 and was almost immediately heralded as a minor classic. As a child, Golding had read enthusiastically R. M. Ballantyne's much beloved *Coral Island* (1858), a flag-waving tale about stalwart British lads who, shipwrecked on a remote and lovely Pacific island, brave adversity with high spirits and bring Christianity to the black natives. Golding found, however, that as an adult, the reading of this children's book had vastly altered for him. Its combina-

Kathleen Woodward, "On Aggression: William Golding's *Lord of the Flies*," *No Place Else: Explorations in Utopian and Dystopian Fiction*, edited by Eric S. Rabkin, Martin H. Greenberg, and Joseph D. Olander, Carbondale: Southern Illinois University Press, 1983, pp. 199–224. Copyright © 1983 by the Board of Trustees, Southern Illinois University. All rights reserved. Reproduced by permission of the publisher.

tion of staunch merriment, arrogance, and naïveté was offensive—worse, dangerous. Although the preface to *Coral Island* declares that the purpose of the book is "fun"—harmless and jolly entertainment—from our perspective in history it is clear to us, as it was to Golding, that this story for children served to rationalize the practice of colonialism and to reinforce the Victorian belief in the cultural, racial, and ethical superiority of the English. Shaken by the atrocities of World War II, the unthinkable mass slaughter organized by Hitler, Golding decided to model a fiction on *Coral Island* which underscored man's inherent capacities for cruelty, not cooperation. *Lord of the Flies*, he has said, is a "realistic" rendering of the hypothetical situation which Ballantyne had proposed one hundred years before. I should also add that it departs radically from the tradition of the romance of survival established by Daniel Defoe's *Robinson Crusoe* (1719) and Johann Rudolf Wyss's *Swiss Family Robinson* (1812–13), which illustrate the enterprising courage of "civilized" man cast away on a deserted island.

Realism Replaces Romance

Just what Golding means by "realistic" is critical here. His vision of evil at the heart of man is violent and dark. When at the end of *Lord of the Flies*, the naval officer who rescues the schoolboys marooned in the midst of an atomic war, says ingenuously, it was like *Coral Island*, wasn't it, we know just how different it has been. The island is going up in flames. The twelve-year-old who had been elected chief is being hunted down in cold blood by the other children. One small child, mulberry-marked by a birthstain, has been lost to carelessness in an earlier fire. Another has been killed by a frenzied mob. A third has been deliberately murdered. In Golding's inversion of Ballantyne's successful survival story, conviviality and high jinks degenerate into shocking savagery as the island turns from a paradise into a fiery warground.

In the beginning, the island is so enchantingly beautiful, peaceful, utopian, that even a twelve-year-old schoolboy is sensitive to its poetic possibilities. As Ralph, the chief, thinks to himself, it is the "imagined but never fully realized place leaping into real life." Uninhabited, rich with fruit, it is the locus of the mundane and the magical: the only limits are those of the imagination. Ralph delightedly perceives the shadows cast on his body by palm fronds as "really green" and the gulls which grace an offshore boulder are to him like "icing on a pink cake." Another central character, Simon, perceives the buds on evergreen bushes as "candles" redolent with spiritual significance. Yet the potential for evil also exists from the beginning, inherent not in the island but in man. In the very first paragraph we learn that the plane which carried the children here in a tragically ironic attempt to shelter them from war, left a "long scar smashed into the jungle." We further read that the first sound which Ralph hears he interprets as the "witch-like cry" of a red and yellow bird. And in the quick course of the story, the delicate pink spiral of the conch, a fragile shell which Ralph first uses to call the scattered kids together and which comes to stand for a democratic form of government and respect for the individual, is smashed, supplanted by the bloody, decaying head of a sow, matted with hungry flies, the emblem of despotism and the perverse desire for gratuitous violence. . . .

A Pessimistic View of Human Nature

What is the lesson which Golding intends for us in *Lord of the Flies?* The purpose of the book [according to Golding] is "to trace the defects of society back to the defects of human nature." It is an argument against the optimistic notion, prevalent for many decades prior to World War II and shared by people of many persuasions, that violence done by man to man could be rooted out by the appropriate form of social machinery. *Lord of the Flies* provides blunt answers to the central and time-honored questions of political theory. Is man basically inherently good or selfish? Altruistic and peaceful, or aggressive and violent? To what extent is human nature fixed? To what extent can human nature be molded by society?

It is my understanding that the fundamental characteristic of utopian literature is social criticism: it embodies a critique of existing social organization. Utopian works make critical statements in fictional, or nonfictional, form about our social values, practices, and institutions. . . .

But if we define dystopian literature, like utopian literature, as primarily a vehicle for social criticism, in what way can we consider *Lord of the Flies* dystopian? Much of the book is devoted to politics, to the competing values of a totalitarian or democratic system. But Golding is not basically critical of the democratic form of government, which was of course his own when he wrote *Lord of the Flies*. Instead his vision is politically conservative, even reactionary. If both utopian and dystopian literature are moved by the impulse that social change is possible and necessary, *Lord of the Flies* is not. For Golding believes that the bottom line, the limiting factor, is human nature, of which he has a bleak and pessimistic view. Man is inherently evil and weak, and human nature is fixed, make no mistake about it. It is only in this sense that we could say that *Lord of the Flies* is dystopian: it is not self-consciously dystopian with regard to a historical moment of a social system, but rather pessimistic with regard to the nature of the human species. But a better term—and here I agree with Golding—would be "realistic." For essentially Golding is warning us that it *can* happen here, that the calculating aggression of a Hitler could erupt in England, or anywhere else or at any time, no matter what the shape of society. What can we do to avert such a tragedy? Golding explicitly counsels humility and self-knowledge as antidotes to the disease of cultural and personal arrogance. We must beware of those who assert, as does the petty tyrant Jack, "'We're not savages. We're

English; and the English are best at everything,'" for such an attitude leads to colonialism, racism, and genocide. But as we will see, *Lord of the Flies* also suggests, implicitly, another means of containing such violence.

Although *Lord of the Flies* does not offer social criticism with the purpose of changing society, it does present a programmatic view of the relationship between human nature and the shape of society. Like utopian and dystopian writing, it demands that we think clearly and critically about our form of politics and the nature of the human animal; it requires that we move our thought beyond the work itself as literature, a fictional world that refers primarily to itself and the creative process, and into the real world of politics. Since it self-consciously presents us with a model of that world, we are both urged and obliged to test it against that world and other models of it in order to assess its use for us at our particular point in history. It is this approach, rather than a formalistic approach, which I believe will yield the best results if *Lord of the Flies* is considered first and foremost a fable.

However, this does raise a thorny theoretical problem. In order to approach *Lord of the Flies* as a dystopian work, or a programmatic work, we must suspend its literary nature and treat it as if it were presenting us a model of society with the purpose of arguing a particular position with respect to it. How do we respond to argument? With argument. By asking if its claims are true or false. With *Lord of the Flies*, therefore, we would first question the adequacy of Golding's model and secondly the truth of his conception of human nature, just as if we were appraising a scientific experiment....

The Tribal Community

Aptly described as an anthropological passion play, *Lord of the Flies* is an inquiry into the politics of cohesion and conflict which attempts to show how the social bond disintegrates and eventually explodes into war. Golding's acute differentiation of

Scene from the 1990 film adaptation of William Golding's Lord of the Flies. *Castle Rock/ Columbia/The Kobal Collection/The Picture Desk, Inc.*

the social roles of the four major characters invites comparison with the four-member hunting team of a primitive tribe as it is portrayed in John Marshall's classic ethnographic film *The Hunters* and analyzed by the cultural historian William Irwin Thompson. According to this research, a successful hunting team in a tribal community requires four men, each of whom play different roles but all of whom work closely together. Thompson suggests that the team can be considered the anthropological germ cell, the primary human group, from which quantum leaps in cultural organization originated. . . . He implies that politically it is superior because it encourages (indeed, demands) the development of individual talent in an atmosphere of cooperation, not competition. Extreme division of labor is not institutionalized, information is shared equally, and the members of the team respect each other's skills. . . .

[The four main characters in *Lord of the Flies* correspond to the four members of a hunting team.] Ralph is the *Head-*

man, the leader who is the person best suited for the position but also the equal of the others. Once given the authority, he shows genuine leadership, learning to assess his limitations and to seek good counsel. As the plot progresses; his sense of responsibility and reality—that is, disillusionment—grows.

Piggy is the *Clown*, the most intelligent of the four and the voice of common sense.

Simon is the *Shaman*, whose religious sensibility and insight into the dark interior of man's nature are essential to the community. It is Simon who grasps both the literal and metaphorical meaning of the beast—the Beast from the Sea is a dead man who is feared, as we must fear our own potential for violence—and who tries to impart this to the others.

Jack is the *Hunter*, intent, obsessive, skillful, and possessed of stamina.

Whereas Thompson views his model of the primitive community as utopian, Golding's fiction of the anthropological primal scene is pessimistic. The origins of human society, he implies, are rooted in conflict, because human nature is basically evil. The important point for us here is that while the spectrum of Golding's characterization corresponds to that portrayed in *The Hunters*, the *structuring* of their activity does not. What goes wrong? Must things break up? The problem is not that the psychological make-up of the four boys is deficient, that they each lack something essential. Rather, Golding's theory of the "essential illness" in human nature which existed from the beginning and which inevitably erupts in violence can be submitted to a structuralist critique. The point is that in *Lord of the Flies* the social bond did not exist from the start (nor is there any real reason for it to exist) and that Golding presents us with a completely unrealistic model of the origins of human politics. Furthermore, Golding does not so much show us how a state of peace under a rational form of government breaks down, as he shows us how the conceivably pleasant condition of anarchy disintegrates under the pressure of aggression. . . .

Omissions Weaken Argument

If Golding's fable is brilliant in what it includes—his characterization is remarkably discerning—it is also ruthless in what it excludes. As a microcosm of the world at large, it self-consciously eliminates crucial aspects of society which create tension but, more importantly, provide purpose and generate binding social structures in the process.

First, Golding dismisses the basic problem of scarcity, which necessitates the organization of work. Fruit and fresh water are abundant, and the climate is tropical. The island is a leisure world where habits of discipline are superfluous. While the younger children play at the sea's edge, the older children play at being grown up. Voting and the right to free speech, the paraphernalia of democracy, are toys to them. The kids have only one urgent task—to keep the rescue fire going—and even this they are incapable of doing, for with few exceptions, their sense of the future gives way to instant gratification. Essentially they are playing a waiting game, and they invent dangerous games to pass the time.

Perhaps even more significant than Golding's bracketing of the problem of scarcity is his choice of a homogeneous group of middle-class white children, all of whom are boys, as a representative cross-section of society. There is no racial tension, no sexual tension, no tension of cultural difference. By populating his story with young boys only, all twelve and under, Golding removes the fundamental adhesive of society—the family. There are no kinship structures whatsoever, no bonds of love or even close friendship among these boys. It is tragically ironic that none of the boys are related by blood—and are eventually polarized by the desire to shed it. Thus the "society" which Golding portrays is *not* a society, but rather a collection of people. It has no objective (other than to prepare its own rescue, and not everyone agrees to that). It cannot even reproduce itself. It is small wonder that it turns pathological.

But this was not Golding's purpose. He intended to show that violence in society arises out of man's very nature, his instincts. Firmly believing that violence is congenital, "the terrible disease of being human" and not the result of faulty social organization, Golding makes no apologies for the parameters of his fiction. As he explains in "Fable": "The boys find an earthly paradise, a world, in fact like our own, of boundless wealth, beauty and resource. The boys were below the age of overt sex, for I did not want to complicate the issue with that relative triviality. They did not have to fight for survival, for I did not want a Marxist exegesis [interpretation]. If disaster came, it was not to come through the exploitation of one class by another. It was to rise, simply and solely out of the nature of the brute." These are strict limits indeed, and they limit the strength of Golding's argument. From our vantage point in history, we know that scarcity remains a basic source of conflict. We would be foolish to think it is not. The energy crisis is real and will only worsen in the future (but we must remember that Golding published *Lord of the Flies* in the fifties when the West was experiencing an efflorescence of consumer goods and the rebuilding of economies crippled during the war was proceeding at an astonishing pace). Whether we agree with Golding that the sexual drive is a "relative triviality" in terms of widespread violence is a more complicated issue to adjudicate, but we can certainly conclude that he does not approach it with sophistication, choosing instead to dismiss it summarily.

The Consequences of Social Failure

But what does Golding mean when he says violence arises "simply and solely out of the nature of the brute"? In part,

Golding has misread the moral of his own fiction. The moral of the story, he has said, is that "the shape of society must depend on the ethical nature of the individual and not on any political system." First, on the contrary, *Lord of the Flies* dramatizes, with power, how a society—like our own, not like a tribal community—can degenerate into lawlessness when there seems to be no apparent need to work with each other, no kinship ties binding people together, and no long-range social purpose but instead an emphasis on immediate satisfaction. Affluence, as we have seen, brings its own dangers. And secondly, it is more accurate, I think, to read *Lord of the Flies* as an argument for strict law and order within the democratic system rather than as a resigned plea that the shape of society depends on the upstanding ethical nature of a few individuals.

To the kids, it appears at first that the situation is ideal. They find themselves liberated from the constraints of their own culture—the adult world—and are able to invent, or so it seems, the form of law and order they wish. "'No grown ups!'" exults Ralph, as "the delight of a realized ambition overcame him." But there is no longer any such thing as the origin of the state, or a clean cultural slate, or the noble savage, only another beginning. Neither cultural tradition nor the instinct for aggression (which is another form of human heritage that I will turn to later) is absent. The boys bring with them the knowledge of a democratic form of government, as they do a taste for violence. The conflict, which Golding so superbly articulates, is between the order of democratically arrived at rules and the expression of aggressive instincts.

There is no question that to Golding's mind democracy is the preferred form of government. He presents it as humane and wise, as infinitely preferable to the insanities of an authoritarian regime....

Golding's view of a democratic form of government is itself naive and innocent. It is clear to us that, unjust as it is, democracy in its "pure" form is not hardy enough to contain aggression. The moral to be drawn from the story is that the sweet persuasions of democracy must be sharpened by force. When Ralph asks Piggy midway through the narrative, "'What makes things break up like they do?'" Piggy's response is deadly accurate. "'I expect it's him,'" he answers, "'Jack.'" Although Golding suggests that everyone has the potential for letting blood—all of the children participate in the killing of Simon—Jack has a greater lust for it than the others. His regime is built on repression and violence. It cannot be combatted with the peaceful measures of democracy. Reason, indignation, and self-assertion, all of which Ralph try, will not work. Near the end of the story when Ralph goes up the mountain to demand Piggy's spectacles and to urge Jack and his band to help maintain the rescue fire, we know Ralph is being naive. He goes unarmed, underestimating the pathology of power.

Nor will the politics of isolation work. Piggy, Ralph, and the twins Sam and Eric try to hold down "civilization" and look after the little ones on the beach, but they are raided by Jack and his hunters, who have established a fort above them. The analogy to this is civil conflict or international war. One must fight back. Aggression requires aggression. But this Ralph never quite realizes. His form of government is constantly on the defensive, and thus he allows the situation to skid out of control. Ralph experiences a growth in moral consciousness—and this makes him sympathetic to us—but not a honing of his sense of *realpolitik* [politics based on practical, material matters]. A curtain flaps sporadically in his brain, as his hold on reality goes dumb and he loses the power of speech.

The only way that the *force* of reason can prevail is to smash Jack's political machine, which involves us in an unpleasant contradiction that Golding does not face (England was forced to go to war against Hitler, and Golding would certainly agree that such action was required). Thus, on Golding's coral island, it is not that the shape of society must depend on the ethical nature of the individual but that the ethics of the democratic system must be bent in order to perpetuate that system. Institutions of discipline and punishment must be erected. In the course of the narrative Jack turns into a [murderous cult leader] Charles Manson or [a brutal Ugandan despot] Idi Amin who should be hunted down as a public enemy, assassinated by a [U.S. intelligence agency] CIA, or incarcerated in a penal colony. At one point, during a meeting, Ralph shouts in exasperation to Jack, "'You're breaking the rules!'" Jack responds, "'Who cares?'" And Ralph can only answer, "'Because the rules are the only thing we've got!'" He's right, but the problem is that there are not *enough* rules: a system of rules is necessary for when the rules are broken.

Those rules come from the adult world, which is absent. Without them and the power to enforce them, incipient democracy breaks down. Jack, the leader of the hunters, is the first to draw a knife to slice into animal flesh, but initially something holds him back—"the unbearable blood." This inhibition, this taboo, this remnant of custom, quickly fades. . . .

Ralph and Piggy, the two characters who steadfastly support democracy and refer to their upbringing in England positively, believe that the adult world provides appropriate models of behavior, and though they are partly naive about this too, they are basically right. Ralph's standard is "the memory of his sometime clean self." He invents a kind of fairy tale about adults *for* children, daydreaming of the cottage on the moor where he lived with his parents before he was sent away to school: there were wild ponies, cornflakes with cream and sugar, and good books to read. What sustained this "utopian" middle-class environment was discipline and English tradition, as well as love. "'Grownups know things,'" Piggy remarks elsewhere. "'They ain't afraid of the dark. They'd meet and have tea and discuss. Then things would be alright.'" It's possible. Realism and maturity might help one to see clearly, diplomacy might work. And we add, if they don't, institutions of punishment exist to repress undesirable behavior. It is in this sense that the political implications of *Lord of the Flies* are conservative, as they always are when someone believes that human nature is basically evil. Given the story, we are forced to conclude that law and order are the prime political issues and that it is better to impose and accept tradition than ever allow the rules to go slack.

Role of Biology and Politics

Since Golding's vision of human nature implicitly sets a limit to political possibilities, we should not only look carefully at how his fictional world corresponds to the world as we know it, but also test it against scientific theory and research. . . .

Although the field of ethology [the study of animal behavior] has been enriched by the contributions of many prominent scientists . . . here I will trace only some of the salient features of the theory of Konrad Lorenz, the famed and prolific Austrian ethologist. Lorenz views the human species as subject to the same laws of causal behavior, that is, natural laws, as are other species. . . . Aggression is natural to man, not unnatural or irrational. This does not mean that Lorenz is sanguine [cheerful, optimistic] about the increasing tempo of international violence. On the contrary, he regards it historically, as a pathological deterioration of behavior mechanisms which originally possessed survival value. From his point of view, what happened on Golding's coral island presumably would not have taken place in a simple tribal community, but only later, after the relationship between the biological basis of human behavior and cultural determinants of human behavior became unbalanced. Lorenz would argue that man was not born in "original sin," but rather that these aberrations of human behavior developed later. Indeed, he has undertaken the study of the relationship between the aggressive instinct, cultural development, and social behavior because he believes that if we understand the extent to which our behavior is innate, not learned, we may well be able to temper the expression of that aggression, which he regards as the greatest danger we face today.

What are the natural causes of the aggressive drive in the human species as well as in other animal species? How does this drive enhance survival? Lorenz advances several answers. The most important function of intra-species aggression is the calibration of the relationship between populations and resources (territoriality). Aggression also contributes to strengthening the defense of the young and furthering sexual selection (the fighting of sexual rivals helps promote selection of the best and strongest animals for reproduction). How is aggression expressed?... Like other species, homo sapiens also has an innate aggressive drive toward its own members but, as Lorenz shows, our cultural and technological development unfortunately has permitted us to release that drive in ways which threaten our survival rather than enhance it. In particular, the invention of weapons long ago upset the balance between social inhibitions and the potential for killing, and as a consequence, it is only the human species that practices mass slaughter of its own kind for no apparent reason.

In *Lord of the Flies* we see this enacted on a small scale. Had Jack and Ralph been limited to fighting out their battle with only their fists as weapons, the consequences of aggressive behavior would have been far less serious—a broken arm perhaps, or a black eye. But Jack and his hunters have introduced two deadly technologies into their war games—the military organization of men, a pentagon of power which Jack mobilizes to search the island for Ralph, and the fire-sharpened spear, which was first directed at the sow and is now intended for Ralph. The atomic war which serves as a backdrop to the manhunt reveals even more clearly the insane disproportion between man's aggressive instinct and his technology for expressing it.

Lorenz observes, however, that the development of weaponry, which made killing easier, has been paralleled by the development of rational responsibility, a specific inhibitory or compensatory mechanism whose purpose is to prevent the abuse of weaponry. Like the aggressive drive, these inhibitions also have an emotional, or instinctive, base. . . .

These instinctive, emotional reactions against intra-specific aggression we see in every member of the island's elite except Jack. When Jack starts to beat Piggy up, hitting him first in the stomach and then on the head, we read that "passions beat about Simon on the mountain-top with awful wings." And the memory of the crazed ritual dance of death, the murder of Simon, revolts Piggy and Ralph, and Simon and Eric too.

But why are their instinctual, emotional responses unable to contain Jack's violence?. . . Lorenz singles out two other contemporary phenomena which discourage the expression of altruism, both of which are at work in *Lord of the Flies*— absolute tolerance of behavior and the lack of positive parental guidance. In part, what little order does exist on the island disintegrates because of the complete tolerance of destructive behavior: no one publicly assumes the responsibility for the loss of the mulberry-marked little boy, and no one publicly acknowledges the killing of Simon. And the "blessing," as Lorenz calls it, of "understanding, responsible, and above all, emotionally stable parents" is also lacking.

Given this, Golding's fictional world does mirror the larger world. It conveys with literary power the pathological nature of contemporary aggression. For it is obvious to us that there is no natural need for Jack to hunt down Ralph. There are plenty of resources for all the kids, and no women to fight over. Thus, although Golding invites our disbelief by casting children as adults, this strategy does strengthen the theme of his fable in a very important way. The desire for instant gratification and narcissistic self-absorption we find normal in children, but reprehensible in adults, whom we expect to display a sense of responsibility for others and a concern for the future. Golding's point, and it is well-taken, is that the contemporary world of adults is in fact infantile and regressive, that there are no adults to guide and discipline the adults. . . .

Children Capable of Violence

As a fable *Lord of the Flies* may be about the evil in the human heart, but as a novel it is about the frightening potential of children for violence. This is one of the complicated and fascinating effects of the book. The adult world may indeed be marked by extreme brutality—we remember intermittently that an atomic war is in process—but it seems for the moment infinitely preferable to the violent anarchy of children. For in the course of the narrative our suspension of disbelief is so perfectly manipulated by Golding that we temporarily forget that these characters are in fact children and respond to them as if they were adults. Thus, when they are rescued by a naval officer at the end of the story, and we recognize with a shock that they are children after all, we are willing to accept anything but this, even an atomic war, which now seems less savage than the violent obsessions of young Jack and his followers.

Civilization Is No Protection Against Humanity's Evil Nature

Patrick Reilly

Patrick Reilly, emeritus professor of English at the University of Glasgow in Scotland, is the author of Jonathan Swift: The Brave Desponder *and* George Orwell: The Age's Adversary.

In the following essay, Patrick Reilly suggests that it is a mistake to read Lord of the Flies *as a book about civilization versus savagery. The ending of the book does not bring salvation for the boys—the civilization they are being returned to is a world at war. Golding's message is that evil resides within the heart of man. Society and civilization do not have the power to cure this innate evil.*

It is facile [too easy] to present [*Lord of the Flies*] as a straight opposition between civilisation and savagery, city and jungle, with Golding upholding the former and all its salutary disciplines against the chaotic free-for-all of the latter. Certainly, this opposition is present but the solution is not nearly so easy as the mere election of one over the other. The first page presents the two states, jungle and Home Counties, which are apparently so remote from each other. The boys are ecstatic at their miraculous relocation. To be on an adult-free, coral island means 'the delight of a realized ambition', conveyed in the 'bright, excited eyes' and 'glowing' faces, the elated boyish exclamations, the sense of glamour and adventure at escaping civilisation. We hear that 'the cause of their pleasure was not obvious', for Ralph, Jack and Simon are at this point

Patrick Reilly, "*Lord of the Flies*: Beelzebub's Boys," *The Literature of Guilt: From "Gulliver" to Golding*, Basingstoke, Hampshire: The Macmillan Press, 1988, pp. 139–61. Copyright © Patrick Reilly 1988. All rights reserved. Reproduced with permission of Palgrave Macmillan.

hot, dirty and exhausted, but that only makes it more plain that internally they feel exhilaratingly emancipated. It is a good island and it is theirs, empty of adult restriction. 'Until the grown-ups come to fetch us we'll have fun.' The island is not to be a permanent home but a storybook holiday.

Idyllic Soon Becomes Infernal

Almost immediately reality breaches the idyll. The marvellous sun burns, the convenient fruit causes diarrhoea, irrational fears come with darkness. The bigger boys deride the littluns' terrors—'But I tell you there isn't a beast!'—but privately they share them. Soon taboos have infiltrated paradise: 'snakes were not mentioned now, were not mentionable'; 'the glamour of the first day' wears increasingly thin. The jungle is now threat rather than playground; even Jack, besotted with hunting, senses that in the forest he shockingly exchanges the role of hunter for hunted, 'as if something's behind you all the time in the jungle'. Ralph is scandalised, but Jack's personal courage is never in question and no one knows better than he the jungle atmosphere. The holiday camp becomes a hellhole as the idyll plummets towards nightmare. 'The best thing we can do is get ourselves rescued.' Life in a real jungle educates the boys to appreciate civilisation: the rescue once so casually postponed is now ardently desired, the missing adult supervision is no longer cause for celebration but grief.

'With a convulsion of the mind', Ralph discovers dirt and decay. Everything breaks down: the shelters collapse, the simplest repairs are too taxing, the basic rules of hygiene are ignored, the habit of disciplined work is lost as lazy, feckless man succumbs to nature. The boys understandably blame this collapse on the absence of adults, but the text denies the reader so simple an explanation. Ralph, Piggy and Simon, left alone as the others slide into savagery, can be forgiven for craving 'the majesty of adult life', for believing that with adults in control none of the insanities would have occurred. Adults, they assure themselves, would not quarrel or set fire to the island; what the boys fail to see is that children are but men of a smaller growth, that the child is father to the man, for they would not be on the island at all but for the fact that adults have quarrelled in an atomic war which may set the whole world ablaze. It is the discovery analogous to that announced by Freud relating to the First World War. The state, which insists on internal peace, is externally the greatest criminal of all; the adults who would make the children behave, handle their own enemies with a sophisticated ferocity that makes Jack look like a mere dabbler in destruction. When the boys pray for a sign from the adult world—'if only they could get a message to us'—their prayer turns into an ambush. A sign came down from the world of grownups'; the dead parachutist descends upon the island and is catalystic in toppling the already disintegrating society into gibbering demon-worship.

Tyranny Versus Democracy

Everything has come full circle. Ralph pines now for the once unheeded benefits of civilisation like a bath or toothbrush, while Simon the prophet can bring Ralph no more joyous tidings than to assure him that 'you'll get back to where you came from'. The island is now a prison, Eden become Gehenna [Jewish equivalent to hell]. Ralph's dreams reflect his altered view of reality and the reversal of priorities which the island experience has produced in him. He turns away from wild Dartmoor and its wild ponies—'the attraction of wildness had gone'; far better 'a tamed town where savagery could not set foot'. *Lord of the Flies* was clearly not written to encourage a flight to the jungle, and the nature it exhibits is certainly very different from that mediated by [William] Wordsworth or [Jean-Jacques] Rousseau. Yet it would be unwise to conclude that it must be a plea for civilisation, at least in its existing form, for, just as clearly, it exposes the delusion that 'civilisation' is civilised and that Jack can only be found in the jungle.

Jack is not a proponent of savage disorder but of stern totalitarian discipline. Far from disliking rules, he loves them
too much and for the wrong reasons: "'We'll have rules!' he
cried excitedly. "Lots of rules! Then when anyone breaks
'em—'" Those critics who find the book upholding Augustine
[fourth-century theologian who developed the concept of
original sin] against Pelagius [heretical theologian who denied
original sin] should reflect that Jack is a confirmed Augustin-
ian with a zest for retribution. From the outset his authoritarianism is glaringly evident. That is why it is such a disas-
trous concession when Ralph, to appease his defeated rival,
tells him that 'the choir belongs to you, of course'. Jack, as
leader of the hunters, becomes invincible as the lord of the
food supply. The need to hunt and kill leads to the formation
of an army and the democratic process is undermined by this
alternative power-structure. Ralph's bitterness when he lashes
the hunters for throwing away a chance of rescue should include himself as target, for he is not blameless. Nor does he
emerge with credit from his showdown with Jack, for he finds
the lure of meat as irresistible as anyone else. His resolve to
refuse the costly meat crumbles and he is soon gnawing as vo-
raciously as the others. It is a crucial victory for Jack, as his
triumphant cry announces; 'I got you meat!'

This is not, as is sometimes mistakenly said, a slide from
society into savagery, but the replacement of one kind of society by another. Jack's exultant claim is the announcement of a
new totalitarian contract in which freedom is the price of
meat. The Grand Inquisitor [of Fyodor Dostoevsky's *The
Brothers Karamazov*] (who was certainly not advocating a return to nature) declared that men will fall down and worship
anyone who guarantees to feed them and his chief complaint
against Christ is that he will not use food to secure obedience.
Jack would have won the Grand Inquisitor's approval. The
provision of meat becomes a key element in the establishment
of his new society. The democrats can stay and get diarrhoea

with Ralph or defect to Jack and a full table, at the trifling cost of their freedom. The meat-giver wins hands down; a hungry democracy cannot compete with a well-fed tyranny. . . . Even Ralph and Piggy, all their free principles notwithstanding, are driven by hunger towards Jack's camp where he sits among piles of meat 'like an idol'. The dictator, as lord of the feast, contemptuously permits the shamefaced pair to eat. When, later, the quarrel rekindles and Ralph attacks them for running after food, Jack needs only to point to the accusatory bone still in Ralph's hand. . . .

Civilization Masks Hidden Savagery

Those who cite the book as proof of how people, removed from the ramparts and reinforcements of civilisation, so easily regress into savagery, have failed to see that, for Golding, our much vaunted civilisation is little more than a sham in the first place. 'We're English; and the English are best at everything.' Such hubris is asking to be chastised and the book duly obliges. Our alleged civilisation is, at best, a mere habit, a lethargy, a conditioned reflex. Jack, longing to kill the piglet yet unable to do so, is simply unlearning a tedious half-taught lesson; three chapters later he has overcome the rote indoctrination as he sniffs the ground while he tracks his prey, obsessed with a lust to kill, more avid for blood than for meat. The island, like a truth-serum, makes us tell the truth about ourselves, the truth that hitherto lay hidden within—it is, in the etymological sense, an education, and its prime lesson is to confirm [Ernest] Renan's belief that we are living on the perfume of an empty vase. Roger is simply the most frightening instance of the emptiness of civilisation; to say that he retreats from it misleadingly implies that he was ever there at all. But the island does not change people so much as liberate them to be their real selves. Jack would be just as arrogant in England, though his aspiration to command would necessarily take a different route. Roger would have the same sadistic drives at home but the island allows them to be indulged with impunity, as he finds himself in the serendipitous position of a psychopath promoted to chief of police. It is, however, not only in the jungle that psychopaths become chiefs of police.

To begin with, Roger, throwing stones to miss, is still conditioned by a distant civilisation now in ruins. The old taboo is still just barely effective. Lurking darkly behind a tree, 'breathing quickly, his eyelids fluttering', longingly contemplating the vulnerable littlun, so temptingly defenceless, Roger is a masterly depiction of barely controlled perversion. Even Ralph, in the roughhouse of the mock ritual, is not immune from the 'sudden, thick excitement' of inflicting pain on a helpless creature. But what is a shocking, fleeting visitation for Ralph is Roger's permanent condition. It is appropriate that, during the killing of the sow with its explicit sexual overtones, he should be the one to find a lodgement for his point and to force it remorselessly 'right up her ass!' Who else but the pervert should lead those pursuing the sow, 'wedded to her in lust', and, at her death, collapsing 'heavy and fulfilled upon her'? Orgasmic release for Roger is always a matter of hurting someone else.

He is a much more frightening figure than Jack, for whereas the latter's cruelty springs from fear—the unfortunate Wilfred is going to be beaten because the chief is angry and afraid—Roger's sadism is the pure, unadulterated thing, with pleasure as its motive. When he hears the delectable news of Wilfred's beating, it breaks upon him like an illumination and he sits savouring the luscious possibilities of irresponsible authority; it is a sadist's elysium [heaven]—absolute power and a stock of defenceless victims. The rescuing officer arrives just in time to prevent a supplantation, for, as the connoisseur in pain, Roger is already beginning to shoulder the chief aside to practise his hellish craft. Significantly, the sharpened stick meant to take Ralph's life is carried by Roger and not Jack. But we do the island an injustice if we blame it for producing

Roger, for he exhibits, rather, the two ostensibly contradictory truths which the book advances: how far the boys have moved away from civilisation and what a tiny journey it is. By the book's close little Percy Wemys Madison has completely forgotten the talismanic address chanted throughout to console him in his ordeal; it is a sign at once of how perilously fragile the civilised life is and of how thoroughly abandoned it can become.

The Rescue Is No Rescue

Whatever flimsy excuse can be offered for missing the implicit indictment of civilisation recurring throughout the text is irreprievably cancelled by the unmistakable irony of the climax. Yet some readers uncomprehendingly dismiss this as a gimmick, Golding sacrificing the text's seriousness to a piece of sensationalism. The truth is that the final startling change of perspective is integral to the book's meaning. Ralph, fleeing in terror, falls, rolls over and staggers to his feet, 'tensed for more terrors and looked up at a huge peaked cap'. The long desiderated [desired] adult has finally arrived and the bloodthirsty savages seeking Ralph's life dwindle to a semicircle of little boys indulging in fun and games; Jack, from being a manic dictator, is reduced to a dirty little urchin carrying some broken spectacles at his waist. This has been astonishingly misinterpreted as an unprincipled evasion of the problems posed by the fable: the horror of the boys' experience on the island is finally only a childish, if viciously nasty, game; adult sanity has returned and the little devils will have to behave themselves again. Human nature cannot be so irremediably bad if the arrival of one adult can immediately put everything to rights—the problem is, apparently, a mere matter of classroom control.

But such obtuseness in face of the text's irony is inexcusable. Ralph is saved but that does not exempt us from scrutinising his saviour or assessing the fate that awaits the rescued boy. The officer seems a doubtful redeemer; his cruiser and sub-machine gun are the sophisticated equivalent of the primitive ordnance used by Jack and his followers. Killers are killers, whatever their implements, sharpened stick or atomic missile, and it is no more a proof of progress to kill technologically than it is for a cannibal to use a knife and fork—the unkempt savages are the counterparts of the trim sailors, not their opposites. We must be gullible indeed to be taken in by evil simply because it comes to us well groomed and freshly, laundered. The officer stands embarrassed as Ralph weeps— English boys should surely behave better than this—but this merely betrays his imperception, which is replicated in that of certain critics. Ralph, weeping for the end of innocence and the darkness of man's heart, is weeping for all men, the officer and his crew included. Because the officer cannot see this does not entitle the reader to be equally blind. The idea that when the cruiser arrives the beast slinks back abashed into the jungle to wait for the next set of castaways is so preposterous that it scarcely deserves refuting.

Concerned with Human Defects

There is no happy ending nor anything optimistic about the final scene. Whatever we may wish, it is not legitimate to infer from the text that society, the *polis*, is man's salvation. The book is not an implicit tribute to the humanising power of social institutions nor does it offer us the city as a refuge from the jungle. Perhaps the city *is* essential, but it very much depends what kind of city it is—Cain's city will not help us. If man regresses in nature, that does not mean that social man is necessarily good; Swift detests the Yahoo but abhors the 'civilised' Yahoos of London and Dublin even more. Of course, man needs a structured community in which to develop his humanity; of course, the city should be the safe and decent haven. But 'should' is not 'is'; in *King Lear* the castle is where man should be safe, the wild heath where he should be endangered, but Lear and Gloucester do not find it so. Golding likewise knows that all too tragically in our century the city itself has become, paradoxically, a jungle, the wild place in which man finds himself born. In any case, Golding's concern is with the defects of man and not those of society, because man is more important than society. Simon is again the decisive figure, for, while not anti-social, he cannot ultimately be defined in social terms—when he goes apart from his fellows to meditate alone, Golding is affirming the superiority of man to men.

Even Children Are Innately Corrupt

Paul Slayton

Paul Slayton was a professor of education at Mary Washington College in Virginia and an expert on censorship and intellectual freedom.

In the following article, Paul Slayton calls Lord of the Flies *William Golding's parable of life in an age where man's technological maturity has outstripped his moral maturity. He argues that* Lord of the Flies *is a paradigm for modern civilization. From Slayton's perspective, Golding deliberately uses children in his novel to show that there is no innocence in childhood—violence is inherent in the very nature of humans. Golding builds the violence in the novel as the children move from killing the sow to killing other children.*

*L*ord of the Flies is William Golding's parable of life in the latter half of the twentieth century, the nuclear age, when society seems to have reached technological maturity while human morality is still prepubescent. Whether or not one agrees with the pessimistic philosophy, the idiocentric psychology or the fundamentalist theology espoused by Golding in the novel, if one is to use literature as a "window on the world," this work is one of the panes through which one should look.

The setting for *Lord of the Flies* is in the literary tradition of Daniel Defoe's *Robinson Crusoe* and Johann Wyss's *The Swiss Family Robinson*, and like these earlier works provides the necessary ingredients for an idyllic utopian interlude. A plane loaded with English school boys, aged five through twelve, is being evacuated to a safe haven in, perhaps, Australia to escape the "Reds," with whom the English are engaged in an atomic war. Somewhere in the tropics the plane is forced to crash land during a violent storm. All the adults on board are lost when the forward section of the plane is carried out to sea by tidal waves. The passenger compartment, fortuitously, skids to a halt on the island, and the young passengers escape uninjured.

The boys find themselves in a tropical paradise: bananas, coconuts and other fruits are profusely available. The sea proffers crabs and occasional fish in tidal pools, all for the taking. The climate is benign. Thus, the stage is set for an idyllic interlude during which British fortitude will enable the boys to master any possible adversity. In fact, Golding relates that just such a nineteenth century novel, R.M. Ballantyne's *Coral Island*, was the inspiration for *Lord of the Flies*. In that utopian story the boy castaways overcame every obstacle they encountered with the ready explanation, "We are British, you know!"

Golding's tropical sojourners, however, do not "live happily ever after." Although they attempt to organize themselves for survival and rescue, conflicts arise as the boys first neglect, then refuse, their assigned tasks. As their "'society" fails to build shelters or to keep the signal fire going, fears emanating from within—for their environment is totally nonthreatening—take on a larger than life reality. Vines hanging from trees become "snake things" in the imaginings of the "little'uns." A nightmare amidst fretful sleep, causing one of the boys to cry out in the night, conjures up fearful "beasties" for the others. Their fears become more real than existence on the tropical paradise itself when the twins, Sam 'n Eric, report their enervating experience with the wind-tossed body of the dead parachutist. Despite Simon's declaration that "there is no beast, it's only us," and Piggy's disavowal of "ghosts and things," the fear of the unknown overcomes their British reserve and under Jack's all-too-willing chieftainship the boys' retreat from civilization begins.

In the initial encounter with a pig, Jack is unable to overcome his trained aversion to violence to even strike a blow at the animal. Soon, however, he and his choirboys-turned-hunters make their first kill. They rationalize that they must kill the animals for meat. The next step back from civilization occurs and the meat pretext is dropped; the real objective is to work their will on other living things.

Then, killing begins to take on an even more sinister aspect. The first fire the boys build to attract rescuers roars out of control and one of the younger boys is accidentally burned to death. The next death, that of Simon, is not an accident. He is beaten to death when he rushes into the midst of the ritual dance of the young savages. Ironically, he has come to tell the boys that he has discovered that the beast they fear is not real. Then Piggy, the last intellectual link with civilization, is killed on impulse by the sadistic Roger. Last, all semblance of civilized restraint is cast-off as the now-savage tribe of boys organizes itself to hunt down and kill their erstwhile leader, Ralph, who had tried desperately to prepare them to carry on in the fashion expected of upper middle-class British youth.

That Golding intended *Lord of the Flies* as a paradigm for modern civilization is concretely evident at the conclusion of the work. During the final confrontation at the rock fort between Ralph and Piggy and Jack and his tribe, the reader readily forgets that these individuals in conflict are not adults. The manhunt for Ralph, too, seems relative only to the world of adults. The reader is so inclined to lose sight of the age of his characters that Golding must remind that these participants are pre-adolescents: The naval officer who interrupts the deadly manhunt sees "A semicircle of little boys, their bodies streaked with colored clay, sharp sticks in hand. . . ." Unlike that officer, the reader knows that it was not "fun and games"

Scene from the 1963 film adaptation of William Golding's Lord of the Flies. *Two Arts/ CD/The Kobal Collection/The Picture Desk, Inc.*

of the boys that the naval officer interrupted. The officer does not realize—as the reader knows—that he has just saved Ralph from a sacrificial death and the other boys from becoming premeditated murderers. Neither is the irony of the situation very subtle: The boys have been "rescued" by an officer from a British man-of-war, which will very shortly resume its official activities as either hunter or hunted in the deadly adult game of war.

Golding, then, in *Lord of the Flies* is asking the question which continues as the major question haunting the world today: How shall denizens of the earth be rescued, from our fears and our own pursuers—ourselves? While Golding offers no ready solutions to our dilemma, an understanding of his parable yields other questions which may enable readers to become seekers in the quest for a moral world. Even if one disagrees with Golding's judgment of the nature of human beings and of human society, one profits from his analysis of the problems confronting people today. . . .

Lord of the Flies has earned for itself and its author great critical acclaim. It has also been extolled by teachers for the excitement it can engender in readers and as a work in which the motivation of characters is readily understood by adolescent readers. Despite these accolades for the novel as a work of literary art and as a teaching tool, *Lord of the Flies* has on occasion aroused the ire of would-be censors.

Some have opposed the use of the novel in the classroom because of the use of "vulgar" language. Certain words, notably "sucks," "ass," and the British slang word "bloody," are used. It is patently obvious that there is no prurient motivation behind the author's choice of these words. Not one of these words is ever used outside of a context in which the word appears to be quite naturally the word the character would use. The choir boys may well sing like "angels," as is stated; nevertheless, these are perfectly normal pre-adolescent boys. Given the proclivities of such youth the world over, verisimilitude would be lost had they, amongst themselves, always spoken like angels.

The sexual symbolism of the killing of the sow has also raised some puritanical brows. This violent scene is described in terms which might well be used to describe a rape. Such symbolism is fully justified, however, if the author is to be allowed to make his point that the motivation of the boys, casting away the cloak of civilization, is no longer merely securing food. Rather, they have moved from serving practical needs to an insane lust for working their will upon other creatures. The next step is the slaughter of their own kind.

Objection, too, has come upon that very point: children killing children. One must remind those who object to this violence that this piece of literature is a parable. Children are specifically used to show that even the innocence of childhood can be corrupted by fears from within. Those who would deny Golding this mode of establishing his theme would deny to all authors the right to make their point in an explicit fashion.

The most vociferous denunciation of *Lord of the Flies* has been vocalized by those who have misread the book to the point that they believe it deals with Satanism. The symbolism of the title, which is the English translation of the Greek word "Beelzebub," is surely being misinterpreted by such folk. In fact, theologian David Anderson states unequivocally that "Golding is a Christian writer." Anderson defines the central theme of *Lord of the Flies* as a statement of what it is like to experience the fall from innocence into sin and to experience damnation. Thus, a theologian sees the novel as one dealing with the Christian doctrine of original sin and of the rupture of man's relationship with God! Consequently, one who would attack this novel as an exercise in Satanism assuredly holds an indefensible premise.

Human Nature Is Not the Sole Cause of Social Evils

David Spitz

David Spitz was a political science professor at Ohio State University for more than 20 years. His publications include The Liberal Idea of Freedom *(1964).*

In this viewpoint, David Spitz suggests that William Golding makes the case in Lord of the Flies *that evil is inherent in human nature. Even children in an Eden-like environment will revert to savagery; however, Spitz reminds us, Golding is ignoring the fact that these children came to the island as the products of a twentieth-century British society, with all of its values and mores. The actions of Jack, for instance, can be ascribed to his authoritarian upbringing. Some cultures are more benign than others, and this is what accounts for the presence of good in the world.*

In a statement to the American publishers of his book, Golding described the theme of *Lord of the Flies* as

> an attempt to trace the defects of society back to the defects of human nature. The moral is that the shape of a society must depend on the ethical nature of the individual and not on any political system however apparently logical or respectable.

In a lecture to American students some years later he restated the overall intention of the work as follows:

> Before the Second World War I believed in the perfectibility of social man; that a correct structure of society would produce goodwill; and that therefore you could remove all social ills by a reorganization of society. It is possible that to-

David Spitz, "Power and Authority: An Interpretation of Golding's *Lord of the Flies*," *The Antioch Review*, vol. 30, no. 1, Spring 1970, pp. 21–33. Copyright © 1970 by the Antioch Review Inc. Reproduced by permission of the Editors.

day I believe something of the same again; but after the war I did not because I was unable to. I had discovered what one man could do to another. I am not talking of one man killing another with a gun, or dropping a bomb on him or blowing him up or torpedoing him. I am thinking of the vileness beyond all words that went on, year after year, in the totalitarian states. It is bad enough to say that so many Jews were exterminated in this way and that so many people were liquidated—lovely, elegant word—but there were things done during that period from which I still have to avert my mind lest I should be physically sick. They were not done by the head-hunters of New Guinea, or by some primitive tribe in the Amazon. They were done, skilfully, coldly, by educated men, doctors, lawyers, by men with a tradition of civilization behind them, to beings of their own kind. . . . I must say that anyone who moved through those years without understanding that man produces evil as a bee produces honey, must have been blind or wrong in the head. . . . I believed then, that man was sick—not exceptional man, but average man. I believed that the condition of man was to be a morally diseased creation and that the best job I could do at the time was to trace the connection between his diseased nature and the international mess he gets himself into.

An Eden-like Setting

To realize his purpose Golding patterned his book after a nineteenth century work on a related theme, R. M. Ballantyne's *The Coral Island*, whose three characters carried the same names as some of the protagonists in *Lord of the Flies*. In this way, he thought, he could show that little had changed though much had changed in that century. He chose British schoolboys because, as he said, he knew them best—he had himself been a schoolmaster for many years—and because they were the stuff of which British gentlemen were made; hence it was to be expected that they would know how to conduct themselves. As Jack said: "We're not savages. We're English; and the English are best at everything. So we've got to do the right things."

He removed them from civil society and isolated them on a remote island, an earthly paradise, beautiful and with an abundance of food, water, and the materials for shelter. He kept them below the age of overt sex, for he wished to exclude this issue as a causal factor. He excluded, too, private property and the struggle for survival—neither work nor robbery was essential for existence—and hence avoided the controversy that engaged [Eugen] Dühring and [Friedrich] Engels over the Robinson Crusoe story: whether political power (force) or economic power (exploitation) should be given the higher priority. Along with [Sigmund] Freud and [Karl] Marx and [Charles] Darwin, he banished Caesar; for there was no danger of external aggression and hence no need for an army. Finally, there were no classes, no divisions, no inequalities based on previous status; except for Jack, who initially appears as the head of a group of uniformed choirboys, a relationship and a dress that are quickly terminated, the only significant sign of difference is that of age.

Everything, then, was there for a calm and peaceful and contented life. It was a veritable utopia: "Here at last was the imagined but never fully realized place leaping into real life." It was, if you will, a state of nature inhabited by free and equal individuals. If anything were to go wrong, as it tragically did, it could only come, then, from within; the only enemy of man was himself.

Golding's magnificent evocation of this world, and of its destruction, constitutes his story, which is too familiar to require retelling here. That it is a literary triumph, that it is politics through literature, no one doubts. I wish now to suggest that it is also a direct and incisive work in political theory.

The Role of Power

One of the many questions that has plagued political thinkers throughout the ages is the question of the legitimacy of power. In every society known to man, some men exercise power over others. Some issue commands that others are expected to obey. But when we look at those who command, it is not immediately evident that they and not some others should occupy the seats of power. They are not all wiser or better, more intelligent or more informed, richer or stronger, than the rest of us. Why then should *they* stand at the top, rather than kneel at the base, of the ever-existing pyramids of power? What makes this right? What makes their retention and exercise of power legitimate?

The quest for this principle of legitimacy is the quest for authority. We obey the policeman, or the tax collector, or the sanitation inspector, not because he has persuaded us of his superior wealth or might or intelligence, but because we recognize his authority. His power is a function of his authority, not the reverse. Hence we need, and have long sought for, a principle other than power that will make power right.

It is a commonplace that this quest has yielded a plenitude of answers. Authority, it has been said, comes from God; so proclaimed the prophet Samuel when he anointed Saul king of the ancient Hebrews. Authority comes from reason; so said Socrates when he insisted that philosophers ought rightfully to be kings, or at the very least counselors to kings. Authority comes from consent; so said [philosophers Thomas] Hobbes and [John] Locke and [Jean-Jacques] Rousseau and the fathers of the American Republic. Authority comes from might; so said, and still say, the victors in every war. Which of these, not to speak of other claims, shall we heed? Which is right? How shall we know?

This is the political problem squarely confronted in *Lord of the Flies.* Consequently it is as representatives or symbols of these diverse responses to the question of authority that I would respond to Golding's leading personages. And it is as a considered answer to this question that I would interpret and apply the moral of his fable.

Simon Is Christ

Simon, it is clear, is the Christ-figure, the voice of revelation. He is "queer" but "always about." He sees the bushes as candles, unlike Ralph who thinks "they just look like candles," or Jack the materialist who dismisses them because they can't be eaten. He was one of the original choirboys, like Peter a member of a group of believers (or apparent believers) and then a defector. He goes into the jungle to pray, to build a church; "he knelt down and the arrow of the sun fell on him." He alone speaks to the beast, the Lord of the flies, and learns that the beast is not something outside of man but is an actual part of man, always close to man, and hence not something to be killed or run away from. Indeed, he had been the first to anticipate this: "Maybe there is a beast. . . . Maybe it's only us." He alone does not fear the false god, the messenger from heaven, the slain airman—a metaphor for history—who is dead but won't lie down. Ralph and Jack see him but turn and run away before discovering his true identity. Simon sees him and understands; he knows that "the beast was harmless and horrible; and the news must reach the others as soon as possible." Like Moses, then, he comes down from the mountain bearing the truth—which in Simon's case is that the beast is Man himself, the boys' (and man's) own natures. But when he comes out of the darkness, bringing the truth, he is not heard—for what ordinary man can live with so terrible an understanding? Like Jesus, he is killed, even though, again like Jesus, he had foreknowledge of his death. "Then the clouds opened and let down the rain like a waterfall." The heavens wept. And with his death the truth he carried died too; for then the parachute-borne figure on the mountain rose and spun and fell into the deep waters. And on the beach:

> The water rose further and dressed Simon's coarse hair with brightness. The line of his cheek silvered and the turn of his shoulder became sculptured marble. . . . Softly, surrounded by a fringe of inquisitive bright creatures, itself a silver

shape beneath the steadfast constellations, Simon's dead body moved out towards the open sea.

Thus men, Christian men, even—as [Fyodor] Dostoevsky's Grand Inquisitor would have understood—those who had once worn priest-like robes, reject the authority and the truth of revelation. They dance and chant and kill; they revel in their passionate joys; they exercise power; but they do not heed the voice of God.

Piggy Is Socrates

Piggy I take to be Socrates, the voice of reason. Like Socrates, he is ugly, fat, and—to men unappreciative of reason—a bore, with a disinclination for manual labor. He is the "outsider." He alone shows marks of intelligence; he can think; he has brains. He not only thinks; he knows himself as well as other men. "I done some thinking. I know about people. I know about me. And him." When he wears his spectacles he can see; he is like Plato's philosopher who has emerged from the cave. Those same spectacles not only shed light; they make possible the lighting of the fire which is meant to be seen. And when he is deprived of those spectacles, he loses his rationality too. He has a sense of what is required for society. He calls for order and justice—"put first things first and act proper"—and appeals to what is right. Though Ralph discovers the conch, it is Piggy who understands its significance as a symbol of legitimacy, an instrument of reason and order. It is Piggy who advises Ralph to call meetings so that names may initially be collected and rational alternatives and policies emerge. Like Socrates in the *Phaedo* seeking to remove the child-like fears of Simmias and Cebes, it is Piggy who reminds the others not to act like children but to behave like grown-ups. Above all, it is he who recognizes that there is no beast and no fear— "unless we get frightened of people." All in all, he is indeed "the true, wise friend."

But Piggy too is killed, and with his death all sense, all reason is gone; the ultimate in madness sets in. Authority must be found elsewhere, for men accept reason no more than they do revelation.

Ralph Is Democratic Man

Ralph is democratic man, the symbol of consent. "There was a mildness about his mouth and eyes that proclaimed no devil." He was "set apart" not by virtue or intelligence or other sign of personal superiority—though he may well have been the tallest and strongest of the boys—but by the fact that it was he who had blown and possessed the conch, who had exercised the symbol of legitimacy. Chosen chief by an election, he sought always to maintain parliamentary procedures, to respect freedom of speech, to rule through persuasion, with the consent of the governed. He was not an intellectual, but he "could recognize thought in another." He could gain understanding from Piggy and had "the directness of genuine leadership," as he demonstrated when he consoled and (temporarily) won over the opposition candidate by naming him second-in-command, by putting him in charge of the hunters.

But Ralph too is rejected. The boys secede from his rule; they destroy the conch; and ultimately, their passions inflamed, they seek even to put him to death. Thus consent, like reason and revelation, is abandoned as a principle of authority. The "three blind mice" having been shunted aside, what finally is left is force, naked power. . . .

Jack Is Authoritarian Man

Jack then, is authoritarian man. Like [Adolf] Hitler and [Benito] Mussolini, he came out of an authoritarian tradition; himself a Satanic figure with his red hair and black cape, he was also the leader of a black-capped and black-cloaked gang that marched in step—"something dark [that] was fumbling along"—and followed orders. His "was the voice of one who knew his own mind," and when it was suggested that there ought to be a chief he immediately and arrogantly demanded that position for himself. Defeated in an election, he took command of the hunters, the forces of naked power. "We'll have rules!" he cried excitedly. "Lots of rules! Then when anyone breaks 'em—" But his desire for many controls did not of course extend to controls he disliked, to those over himself. Then he rejected the rules and claimed the right to decide for himself. To Ralph's plea that he had been chosen chief, Jack replied: "Why should choosing make any difference? Just giving orders that don't make any sense—. . . Bollocks to the rules! We're strong—we hunt! If there's a beast, we'll hunt it down! We'll close in and beat and beat and beat—!" He was contemptuous of the masses, dismissing the little ones as "useless." "It's time some people knew they've got to keep quiet and leave deciding things to the rest of us—" Madness came often into his eyes, and when as hunter and warrior he again cloaked himself, this time behind a mask of paint, he lost all inhibitions; "he was safe from shame or self-consciousness"; he gave full vent to his passions. The conch, as Piggy said, was "the one thing he hasn't got"; and when he sought to assert his leadership through its use he blew it "inexpertly" and then, finding that he could not have his way, set it aside "at his feet." Eventually it was shattered by his henchman into a thousand fragments.

Yet he prevailed. "Power lay in the brown swell of his forearms: authority sat on his shoulder and chattered in his ear like an ape."

The Children Are Not Really Saved

Who and what, then, is the Lord of the flies?

He is Beelzebub—a Greek transliteration of the Hebrew Ba'al Zevuv, which means Lord of the flies; or, as it is rendered in some New Testament texts, Beelzebul, which means

Lord of dung, or Lord of a fly-ridden dung heap. As such, he is the personification of evil. He is the beast that is part of man. Having rejected God, man can look only to himself. Having rejected reason and consent, what remains within himself is only savagery and force. The boys are the flies and the beast, the evil, the senseless passion that is in man; in each and every man—in Jack, in Roger, even (under special circumstances) in Ralph and Piggy, even in you and me—is the Lord.

This is possible because the boys live in the dark. In the light they would be ashamed; and he who has common sense, whom—like Ralph—would live in the light, is an outcast. . . .

With the triumph of the Lord of the flies, the darkness in man's heart, Ralph weeps for the end of innocence. But the final, most devastating, most ironic note has yet to be sounded. For at the very moment when Ralph thinks he is saved, when all the children are saved, by the appearance of adults on the island, *we* know that he and they are not really saved. For the man who heads the adults who have come to rescue them is a naval officer, also a leader of hunters; and the ship to which he will take them is a battle cruiser, which cannot carry them back to the safe shore (England), since that shore is now in ruins, but will itself soon be engaged in a hunt for the enemy—man—in the same implacable way as Jack and his deranged followers hunted Ralph. The boys move not from one evil to another evil, but from one aspect or level to another of the same evil; they go from the Lord of the flies writ small to the Lord of the flies writ large. For power based on the authority of force has been supplanted not by a different principle of authority, but only by another, though greater, power based also on the authority of force. And who, or what, will control this greater power?

So the moral remains the same: when all else fails, clubs are trumps. And all else must fail.

Valid Only for Golding's Schoolboys

So, at least, Golding would have it appear. But is this really so? Has Golding proved his case?

His case, let it be recalled, is that evil is innate in man; that even the most suitable environmental conditions, unmarred by all the customary factors that have distracted and corrupted men in the past, will not suffice to overcome man's capacity for greed, his innate cruelty and selfishness; and that those, therefore, who look to political and social systems detached from this real nature of man are the victims of a terrible, because self-destructive, illusion. His method is to create a civilization out of innocence, to detach a group of the best of our very young and to put them into a state of nature, there to found a civil society on such principles of decency as seem to them appropriate, and to follow with a close and careful eye their inevitable course of destruction. His evidences are the events that constituted that course.

Now a novelist is not a historian; much less so is the author of a myth or fable. We cannot submit his work, therefore, to the standards and tests of historical or anthropological research. (For this reason I omit from consideration here what would otherwise be, I think, a telling criticism of Golding's argument: namely, that evil inheres not simply in man but also in collectivities, institutions, and social forces.) But we can judge him by his own method and evidences. And here, while I do not doubt that Golding has called our attention to a profound but partial truth, to what he has strikingly and properly called "the terrible disease of being human," I would contend that—precisely because he has built on but a partial truth—he has fallen short, far short, of establishing his case.

For what Golding has forgotten is that a state of nature is not necessarily a state of political and moral innocence. The boys who inhabited the island did not spring up full-blown, as did Athena from Zeus's head. They were the carefully chosen products of an already established middle-class society. They were socialized in, and were a partial microcosm of, twentieth century English (or Western) civilization; and they had brought that civilization, or what fragments of it they could remember, with them. Hence the values they possessed, the attitudes they displayed, the arrangements they established, and the practices in which they engaged, were all in some degree or other a reflection of the world into which they had been born and within which they had been educated and fashioned.

Jack and the choirboys, for example, had brought with them a system of order based on authoritarianism, and had been habituated to the wearing of masks (their uniforms) which set them apart, and enabled them to act differently from other men. Piggy brought his spectacles, an artificial aid provided by the civil society in which he had lived; and so conditioned had he been by that society that with those spectacles he saw precisely those democratic and middle-class values that that society esteemed, he appealed repeatedly to science and to what grown-ups would think. Maurice, who in his other life "had received chastisement for filling a younger eye with sand," now, despite the absence of a parent who might let fall a heavy hand, felt the unease of wrong-doing when he committed the same act, and hurried away. Even Roger, around whom the hangman's horror was later to cling, was initially bound by the taboos of the old life. He had gathered a handful of stones to throw at a smaller child. "Yet there was a space round Henry, perhaps six yards in diameter, into which he dare not throw. . . . Round the squatting child was the protection of parents and school and policemen and the law. Roger's arm was conditioned by a civilization that knew nothing of him and was in ruins."

Hence we still don't know, any more than we know from the story of Robinson Crusoe, what man, innocent, naked, non-socialized man is really like. We still don't know what is innate and what is environmentally conditioned in man. Nor can we ever hope to attain this sort of knowledge; for the individual apart from society is an inconceivable thing—he is always, no matter how peculiar or unique a person, still a social animal. And if it be said, despite this, that all societies are evil, or that there is evil in all societies, which means that men however created or evolved are necessarily the source of that evil, it is still not shown what in man or in his circumstances produces that evil, or why, and whether this is irredeemable.

Golding's truth, if truth it be, is thus true only for his English schoolboys, and those of like circumstances. It is not necessarily true of the products of other cultures and civilizations, or of other times.

All Societies Are Not Equal

This point merits pursuit. If Golding is right, if "the shape of a society must depend on the ethical nature of the individual," and if that nature is innately evil, then every society must be rooted in naked or arbitrary force; every society must be evil; every society must be, in this sense, the same.

But every society is not the same. Horrors and indecencies abide, to be sure, in every society; but the horrors and indecencies that Golding encountered in the concentration camps of Nazi Germany were outrages of a different degree, perhaps of a different order, than those to be found in some other states. Does this not suggest that the problem of human bestiality is more complex, more factor-bound, than the single-factor explanation Golding makes it out to be? That the customs and traditions of a people, their ethical precepts and practices socialized through education and over time, even perhaps their social and political arrangements, make a difference?. . .

Now Golding has himself admitted that intelligence and historical knowledge are of supreme importance and relevance in meeting [the] problem [of the consequences that readily flow from "the terrible disease of being human"]. It is, he has said, in "that attempt to see how things have become what they are, where they went wrong, and where right, that our only hope lies of having some control over our own future. If this is so, if there is *some* hope of controlling our future, then the hypothesis of innate evil is but partly right, and therefore partly wrong. It cannot by itself explain the governance of mankind.

The matter cannot rest here. Every society does indeed, in some measure at least, rest on force. We may appeal to God, even claim (as we now officially do) that this is a nation "under God." We may invoke the sanction of justice, even claim (as we officially do) that we provide "liberty and justice for all." We may rely on consent, even claim (as we regularly do) that our governors are chosen by the freely recorded and continuing consent of the people, through elections, and that they derive "their just powers from the consent of the governed." But we, along with every other so-called civilized nation, nonetheless maintain an army and police force. Without them, or so it is believed, the state cannot survive, or do the job it purports to do. Without them, or so it is believed, we cannot resist the will of greater powers or impress our will on those with lesser force.

Yet it remains true that while a people may do many things with bayonets, they cannot sit on them. Force alone is not enough: it neither unites the nation that employs it, nor sustains the nation that is formed after its use, nor controls a people that has been subjugated by it. It is, in any case, a base principle, and wholly irrelevant to right; no just man would be content to be hammer, just as he would not be content to be anvil.

We are caught, then, in a pathetic dilemma: we cannot seem to do without force, and in this respect every society runs the risk of being oppressive; but we cannot do without justice, and in this respect force becomes not an end but a means, an instrument in the service of right. But the use of violent means tends always to corrupt the user and may well distort, and render unattainable, the desired end. Suppression even in the service of right is still suppression, and that, if not wrong, is but painfully right.

So we seem to be back where we began. There is power, and there is authority; and how to bring them together in the name of justice—whether of reason, revelation, or consent— may well exceed, if not the imagination, at least the practical capacities of mortal man. This, too, may be a part of the terrible disease of being human.

However, what is perhaps more astonishing is not that there is so much evil in the world but that there is a measure of good; not that there is so much violence but, occasionally, a period or a place that knows a degree of amity and peace; not that there is so much selfishness and greed but, from time to time, a touch of altruism—and it matters not here whether this is called enlightened self-interest or sacrifice—and decency. It is necessary, here as everywhere, to draw distinctions. There are differences of kind as well as of intensity among evils, and among societies in which evils abound. It is undeniably true, for example, that racial and ethnic minorities are basely and unjustly treated in this country [the United States]; but to label this a greater evil than Hitler's policies of genocide and war is to manifest nothing less than moral blindness. It is also true that in our social and political arrangements and practices we are far from realizing our avowed democratic ideals; but to confuse this dreadful failure with the worst practices of totalitarian or repressive systems is hardly an expression of responsible judgment.

This is not to excuse evils, or fatuously [foolishly] explain them away. It is merely to say that while no human society is completely without evil, the fact that there are differences in the levels of evil among societies indicates that factors other than "man" or "evil in man" play an important role. They make a real difference in the quality of human existence. They warrant the hope, expressed by prophets and democratic thinkers, that in principle an ideally good society may be approximated if not attained.

Some societies, some political and social systems, are in fact less vile than others. The evil that is common to them all cannot causally account for that which distinguishes them from each other.

Golding Warns Against Racial and Class Violence in *Lord of the Flies*

Paul Crawford

Paul Crawford is a professor of health humanities in the School of Nursing, Midwifery, and Physiotherapy at the University of Nottingham, England, and the author of the book Politics and History in William Golding.

Paul Crawford suggests in the following essay that Golding's harrowing experiences during World War II inspired him to write of the capacity for racial violence in society. In particular, in Lord of the Flies, *Golding is chastising the complacency of the British, who smugly claimed that the atrocities of Nazism could not have happened in their country. Crawford analyzes Golding's use of fantastic and carnivalesque motifs, which he finds effectively shift perspective and evoke Nazi atrocities.*

In *Lord of the Flies* ... Golding's *Vergangenheitsbewältigung*, or "coming to terms with the past," concludes that the English and Nazis are not so different as one might expect. It is this painful evocation of similitude that has been overlooked in earlier critical readings. [*Lord of the Flies*] should certainly be included in the wider European tradition of "literature of atrocity." That we know Golding himself to have been deeply involved in the war, on intimate terms with its horror, and exercised by expressions not just of Allied moral superiority to Nazis, but of racial violence that broke out in England after the war as well, is significant for a full understanding of his early novels.

Paul Crawford, "Literature of Atrocity: *Lord of the Flies* and *The Inheritors*," *Politics and History in William Golding: The World Turned Upside Down*, Columbia: University of Missouri Press, 2002, pp. 50–80. Copyright © 2002 by The Curators of the University of Missouri. All rights reserved. Reproduced by permission.

In *A Moving Target*, Golding tells of the impact this loss of belief in the "perfectibility of social man" had on *Lord of the Flies*: "The years of my life that went into the book were not years of thinking but of feeling, years of wordless brooding that brought me not so much to an opinion as a stance. It was like lamenting the lost childhood of the world. The theme of *Lord of the Flies* is grief, sheer grief, grief, grief, grief." Despite such commentary from Golding himself, the effect of the war and other social contexts such as racial violence on his writing has drawn scant attention from critics. This emphasis has tended to remain submerged. . . .

The following [reading] of *Lord of the Flies*. . . [is meant] to redress this lack. . . .

Parallels Between Traditions

In *Lord of the Flies*, fantastic and carnivalesque modes are used to subvert postwar English complacency about the deeds of Nazism, particularly the Holocaust. Although oblique, Golding effects an integration between literature and cultural context. This interpretation renegotiates previous critical paradigms that have, for the most part, centered on the timeless or perennial concerns of this novel about a group of English schoolboys, deserted on a South Pacific island following a nuclear third world war, and their descent into ritual savagery and violence. As most critics attest, the characters replicate those in R. M. Ballantyne's *Coral Island* (1858), who in similar straits pull together and overcome external dangers from natives and pirates. Ballantyne's schoolboys exemplify cultural assumptions of imperial superiority and conversely the inferiority of the "fuzzy-wuzzies" or "savages," the indigenous race feared for its cannibalistic practices. For Ballantyne's boys, evil and degenerative nature is outside of them, and the suggestion is that imperial colonialism is beneficent, that the savage can be "saved" by the civilized, Christian Western man. Such inherent and dominant racial elitism is extended in Ballantyne's

Gorilla Hunters (1861), in which older versions of the same schoolboys, on a scientific expedition in Africa, hardly differentiate between the gorillas and the natives.

Golding subverts these notions of racial and cultural superiority, of scientific progress, notions casting long shadows over atrocities against the Jews carried out in World War II. He draws a parallel between the violent history of English imperialist adolescent masculine culture and the extermination of the Jews. He broaches the grim fact that English colonial warfare against "inferior" races, modeled on hunting and pig sticking, was not a million miles away from the extermination of the Jews. . . .

Golding's critique is not directed exclusively at Nazi war criminality but at the postwar complacency of the English who too readily distanced themselves from what the Nazis did. He reminds them of their long infatuation with social Darwinism. [Critic] Graham Dawson maps the trajectory of the "soldier hero," an "idealized," militaristic masculinity at the symbolic heart of English national identity and British imperialism. He argues that this "imagining of masculinity" in terms of warfare and adventure pervades the national culture, swamps boyhood fantasies, and, in particular, promotes rigid gendering, xenophobia, and racial violence. In *Lord of the Flies*, Golding's critique of British imperial, protofascist history is powerfully registered by the Nazification of English schoolboys: "Shorts, shirts, and different garments they carried in their hands: but each boy wore a square black cap with a silver badge in it. Their bodies, from throat to ankle, were hidden by black cloaks which bore a long silver cross on the left breast and each neck was finished off with a hambone frill."

Jack's Gang and Nazism

James Gindin insists that Golding's description of Jack's gang—who are English—"deliberately suggests the Nazis." Despite a preference for the universal aspects of Golding's fiction, Leighton Hodson suggests Piggy might represent the "democrat and intellectual," Jack "Hitler," and Roger a "potential concentration camp guard." L. L. Dickson identifies the novel as political allegory, referring to World War II atrocities, particularly those inflicted upon the Jews. Suzie Mackenzie refers to Jack's gang as a "fascist coup" and sees the opposition between democracy and totalitarianism as one of the novel's themes. The "black" garments and caps are, indeed, highly suggestive of the Nazi *Schutzstaffeln*, or SS—the "Black Angels" responsible for the Final Solution [to the Nazis' perceived "Jewish Problem"]. Certainly, Golding's candid comments to John Haffenden suggest this: "I think it's broadly true to say that in *Lord of the Flies* I was saying, 'had I been in Germany I would have been at most a member of the SS, because I would have liked the uniform and so on.'" They also suggest Oswald Mosley's [founder of the British Union of Fascists] Blackshirts. The silver cross may obliquely bring to mind both the Iron Cross (*Eisernen Kreuz*) and the anti-Semitic swastika. The reference to "hambone" may suggest the skull and crossbones or Death's Head (*Totenkopf*) insignia of the SS. Certainly, the "black cap with a silver badge in it" resembles the black ski caps decorated with the skull and crossbones worn by Hitler's early group of bodyguards, the *Stabswache*. Like Hitler's *Stabswache*, which was made up of twelve bodyguards, Jack's gang or squad is small in number. Nazification of Jack's gang is further amplified by its delight in parades and pageantry, which together with "the unshackling of primitive instincts" and "the denial of reason" is all part of what psychoanalytical theories categorize under the "style and methods of fascism," according to [philosopher] Ernst Nolte. This mingling of Nazism and Englishness is not to be overlooked. Of course, it is the violence of Jack's gang that most powerfully suggests links between them and the Nazis. . . .

Adolescent Male Aggression

Adolescent male aggression . . . is central to Nazism and other versions of fascism or totalitarianism. [German scholar] Silke Hesse contends that because adolescents are "unattached," "mobile," impressionable, physically strong, and easily "directed towards ideals and heroes" on account of unfocused sexuality, the adolescent gang is seen as "a most efficient tool in the hands of a dictator." She concludes: "Of course, Fascism cannot be exhaustively explained with reference to male adolescence. Yet most of the major theories of fascism emphasize the youthful nature of the movement and, even more, its masculinity, in terms both of participation and of traditionally masculine values." . . .

For Golding, the dominant and prevalent cultural assumptions found in Ballantyne's stories support the projection of evil onto external objects or beings, such as savages, and in Nazi Germany's case the Jews. But Golding maintains that the darkness or evil that humans fear, and consequently attempt to annihilate, is within the "civilized" English subject. Importantly, Golding appears to have a specific continuity in mind concerning an evil that is not overcome or displaced by English civilization, but is, in effect, a potential that comes hand in hand with it. He connects adolescent English schoolboys from privileged backgrounds, the imperial scouting ethos, and fascism. Thus, whereas in Germany fascism actually sprouted, while in England it did not, there is nonetheless the possibility that the English ethos could easily tip over into fascism (as it does on the island) since privileged education and scouting ideology have much in common with fascism. In order to rebut Ballantyne's projection of evil onto savages, and to draw attention to the ability of the English—with their schooling in fascistic behavior—to mirror Nazism, Golding uses the combined forces of fantastic and carnival modes.

In *Lord of the Flies*, the world of the island is apprehended from the viewpoint of the schoolboys. Initially, they appear to

Members of the Hitler Youth in Vienna exchange the Nazi salute with a guard watching. Popperfoto/Getty Images.

be all-around empire boys, characters in the island adventure tradition that stretches back to Daniel Defoe's *Robinson Crusoe*, Robert Louis Stevenson's *Treasure Island*, and Ballantyne's *Coral Island*. But their preoccupation with natural phenomena and survival rapidly changes to a preoccupation with the unknown and inexplicable. They face beasts and phantoms in a succession of apparently supernatural events. Uncertain and fearful, the boys are subjected to unexplained phenomena. Suspense and hesitation as to the nature of the "beast" follow, and their fear increases accordingly. Although at first it is only the "littluns" that appear affected by this fear, the circle widens until all the boys, including Ralph and Jack, believe in the "Beast.". . .

Undermining British Complacency

Effectively, the fantastic elements in *Lord of the Flies* operate in tandem with those of carnival: they combine to disturb us and subvert dominant cultural notions of the superiority of civilized English behavior. These are the kind of assumptions that buoyed the complacency of England, and indeed other Allied nations, namely, that the atrocities perpetrated by the Nazis were an exclusively German phenomenon. Within the fantastic framework, it is the break from potential supernatural explanation to the chilling and uncanny reality of natural explanation that disturbs us: that the Beast is human, Nazi-like, and English. We participate in the shock that this shift in perspective brings. Instead of externalizing and projecting evil onto objects, phantoms, and supernatural beasts, we confront the reality of human destructiveness. This is registered in both a universal or "perennial" frame and a specific "contemporary" frame, polemicizing the English capacity for Nazism, especially in the light of its exclusionary class system. Although the novel is set in the future, the surface detail, as discussed by earlier critics such as James Gindin, corresponds to World War II. In effect, the fantastic interrogates the postwar "reality" of Britain and its Allies. Yet it does not do so alone.

The shift from the fantastic to the uncanny amplifies carnivalesque elements in the text that symbolically subvert, turn upside down, the vision of civilized, ordered, English behavior. In combination, these elements are the structures, through which *Lord of the Flies* disturbs. Yet such is the inherent irreversibility of the narrative structure—its dependence upon hesitation or suspense of explanation—that we cannot read *Lord of the Flies* and register the peculiar shock it delivers a second time. Indeed, there is something particularly "evanescent" [fleeting] about the pure fantastic, not as a genre, but as an element. Ultimately, the shock recognition of the negative, transgressive, "evil" side of not simply human behavior but the behavior of English boys is what is disturbing about *Lord of the Flies*. Such shock recognition is effected by the combination of fantastic and carnival elements. Because of the fantastic's evanescence, we need to recall our first reading when we reexamine *Lord of the Flies*: we must remember our initial shock. We find no relief in the novel's coda at the end of the book when the boys are "saved" by an English naval officer. Our unease shifts from the carnival square of the island to the wider adult world—a world at war for a third time, a world in which the theater of war greatly resembles, in its detail of a paramilitary fascist group, machine-gunning and, in its dead parachutist, the familiar Second World War. It is a world of continuing in-humanity. . . . The naval officer marks the gap between ideal British behavior and reality: "'I should have thought that a pack of British boys—you're all British aren't you?—would have been able to put up a better show than that—I mean—.'" The substantiation of the children as British subjects is not superfluous to the novel's meaning. It is fundamental to this novel's ethical interrogation of England, Britain, and its Allies at a specific juncture in history.

Piggy Is a Jewish Figure

One of the most powerful carnivalesque elements in *Lord of the Flies* is that of the pig, which Golding uses symbolically to subvert dominant racial assumptions, in particular toward the Jews, and, universally, toward those humans considered alien or foreign to any grouping. This has alarming relevance to the atrocities committed against the Jews in World War II, yet has been overlooked by Golding critics who have not interpreted Golding's merging of the pig hunt with the human hunt, and the racial significance of eating pig flesh at carnival time.

The pig symbol is developed in *Lord of the Flies* as the pig of carnival time. It is a major motif: as locus of projected evil; as food for the schoolboys; as propitiation to the Beast; but more than anything, as the meat the Jews do not eat. This link between pig flesh and the Jews is reinforced by Golding's choice of the novel's Hebraic title. "Lord of the Flies," or "Lord of Dung," as John Whitley renders it, comes from the Hebrew word *Beelzebub*. [Critics] Peter Stallybrass and Allon White argue that the eating of pig meat during carnival time is an anti-Semitic practice. It is an act of contempt toward the Jews for bringing about the Lenten fast. White asserts: "Meat, especially, pig meat, was of course the symbolic centre of carnival (*carne levare* [Latin for "to take up meat"] probably derives from the taking up of meat as both food and sex)." That the pig becomes human and the human being becomes pig in the frenzied, carnivalistic debauchery of Jack and his totalitarian regime is important. The shadowing of pig hunt and human hunt, ending with Simon's and Piggy's deaths, and almost with Ralph's, signifies the link between the pig symbol and the extermination of those considered alien or outsiders. The name "Piggy" does not merely imply obesity. It is the lower-class Piggy who is always on the periphery of the group of schoolboys, always mocked, never quite belonging. As [English professor] Virginia Tiger points out, "Piggy is killed ... because he is an alien, a pseudo-species." Piggy is alien or foreign, and, as such, he is a focus for violence based on the sort of racial assumptions found in Ballantyne's writing, but it is important to clarify the precise nature of his outsider status. The character name "Piggy" does not, unlike that of Ralph and Jack, feature in Ballantyne's *Coral Island*. Piggy is Golding's creation—a creation that suggests a Jew-like figure: "There had grown tacitly among the biguns the opinion that Piggy was an outsider, not only by accent, which did not matter, but by fat, and ass-mar [asthma], and specs, and a certain disinclination for manual labour". We find something of the Jewish intellectual in this description of the bespectacled Piggy, with his different accent and physical feebleness. The stereotype of Jewish feebleness has been a stock in trade of anti-Semites and peddlers of degeneration theories. It is here that we witness the anti-Semitism of carnival. In essence, Golding utilizes the imperial tradition of pig sticking to suggest a continuum between English imperialism and fascism. . . .

Golding Attacks British Civilization

We may view Golding's use of carnival in *Lord of the Flies* as registering his deeply felt unease about the nature of English "civilization" in light of the events of World War II—of totalitarianism and genocide: a "civilization," among others, that is primed for the total wipeout of nuclear apocalypse. The misrule of carnival in contemporary history is presented as integral not simply to Nazis or other totalitarian regimes but also to England with its divisive and cruel class system. Golding lays bare an alternative view to civilized English behavior, one that counters accepted, familiar, erroneous complacencies. In the isolated focus, in the "carnival square" of Golding's island, carnival affirms that everything exists on the threshold or border of its opposite. In effect, Golding explodes a Nazi-English or them-us opposition.

So, to summarize, noncelebratory or Juvenalian [in the style of Roman poet Juvenal] satire with its combined fantastic and carnivalesque in *Lord of the Flies* subverts the view that the "civilized" English are incapable of the kind of atrocities carried out by the Nazis during World War II. These modes are deployed in the novel as an attack on what Golding deems to be a complacent English democracy, and its masculinity and classist attitudes in particular, in relation to the rise of National Socialism.

The Human Spirit Can Triumph over Barbarism

Bernard S. Oldsey and Stanley Weintraub

Bernard S. Oldsey was a professor of English literature at West Chester University of Pennsylvania and the author of two novels and thirteen works of literary criticism. Stanley Weintraub is a historian, biographer, and professor emeritus of literature at Pennsylvania State University. He was the editor of Shaw: The Annual of Bernard Shaw Studies *and has written twenty books on George Bernard Shaw, among them the award-winning* Journey to Heartbreak: The Crucible Years of Bernard Shaw.

In the following article from Bernard S. Oldsey and Stanley Weintraub's influential critical study of Golding, the authors argue that Lord of the Flies *is neither a parable nor a fable but rather an allegory. It is a social, rather than a religious, allegory of how quickly humankind's savage nature asserts itself when the restraints of civilization are removed. For Oldsey and Weintraub, the book does not end on a pessimistic note, despite the interpretation of many other critics. They cite the fact that three of the four major characters—namely, Ralph, Piggy, and Simon—all reject partially or completely the barbarism of the forces led by Jack as evidence of an optimistic ending.*

Golding's characters, like his setting, represent neither fictional reality nor fabulistic unreality, but, rather, partake of the naturalistic and the allegorical at the same time. As a result, they emerge more full bodied than Kafka's ethereal forms, more subtly shaded than Orwell's animal-farm types, and more comprehensibly motivated than Bunyan's religious

Bernard S. Oldsey and Stanley Weintraub, "Beelzebub Revisited: *Lord of the Flies," The Art of William Golding*, Orlando, FL: Harcourt, Brace & World, Inc., 1965, pp. 13–40. Copyright © 1965 by Bernard S. Oldsey and Stanley Weintraub. All rights reserved. Reproduced by permission of Harcourt.

ciphers. Bit by bit we can piece together fairly solid pictures of the major figures in *Lord of the Flies*. And since a number of commentators have fallen into interpretive error by precipitously trying to state what these characters "mean," perhaps it would be best here to start by trying to state what they "are."

Ralph, the protagonist, is a boy twelve years and a "few months" old. He enters naïvely, turning handsprings of joy upon finding himself in an exciting place free of adult supervision. But his role turns responsible as leadership is thrust upon him—partly because of his size, partly because of his attractive appearance, and partly because of the conch with which . . . he has blown the first assembly. Ralph is probably the largest boy on the island (built like a boxer, he nevertheless has a "mildness about his mouth and eyes that proclaimed no devil"). But he is not so intellectual and logical as Piggy ("he would never be a very good chess player," Golding assures us), not so intuitively right as Simon, nor even so aggressively able to take advantage of opportunity as Jack. For these reasons there has been some reader tendency to play down Ralph as a rather befuddled Everyman, a straw boy of democracy tossed about by forces he cannot cope with. Yet he should emerge from this rites-of-passage *bildungsroman* with the reader's respect. He is as much a hero as we are allowed: he has courage, he has good intelligence, he is diplomatic (in assuaging Piggy's feelings and dividing authority with Jack), and he elicits perhaps our greatest sympathy (when hounded across the island). Although he tries to live by the rules, Ralph is no monster of goodness. He himself becomes disillusioned with democratic procedure; he unthinkingly gives away Piggy's embarrassing nickname; and, much more importantly, he takes part in Simon's murder! But the true measure of Ralph's character is that he despairs of democracy because of its hollowness ("talk, talk, talk"), and that he apologizes to Piggy for the minor betrayal, and that—while Piggy tries to escape his share of the guilt for Simon's death—Ralph cannot be the hypocrite (this reversal, incidentally, spoils the picture often given of Piggy as superego or conscience). Ralph accepts his share of guilt in the mass action against Simon, just as he accepts leadership and dedication to the idea of seeking rescue. He too, as he confesses, would like to go hunting and swimming, but he builds shelters, tries to keep the island clean (thus combating the flies), and concentrates vainly on keeping a signal fire going. At the novel's end Ralph has emerged from his age of innocence; he sheds tears of experience, after having proven himself a "man" of humanistic faith and action. We can admire his insistence upon individual responsibility—a major Golding preoccupation—upon doing what must be done rather than what one would rather do.

Ralph's antagonist, Jack . . . , is approximately the same age. He is a tall, thin, bony boy with light blue eyes and indicative red hair; he is quick to anger, prideful, aggressive, physically tough, and courageous. But although he shows traces of the demagogue from the beginning, he must undergo a metamorphosis from a timidity-shielding arrogance to conscienceless cruelty. At first he is even less able to wound a pig than is Ralph, but he is altered much in the manner of the transformation of the twentieth-century dictator from his first tentative stirrings of power lust to eventual bestiality. Although Golding is careful to show little of the devil in Ralph, he nicely depicts Jack as being directly in league with the lord of flies and dung. Jack trails the pigs by their olive-green, smooth, and steaming droppings. In one place we are shown him deep in animalistic regression, casting this way and that until he finds what he wants: "The ground was turned over near the pig-run and there were droppings that steamed. Jack bent down to them as though he loved them." His fate determined, Jack is a compelled being; he is swallowed by the beast—as it were—even before Simon: "He tried to convey the compulsion to track down and kill that was swallowing him up." Jack's Faustian reward is power through perception. He perceives almost intuitively the use of mask, dance, ritual, and propitiation to ward off—and yet encourage simultaneously—fear of the unknown. Propitiation is a recognition not only of the need to pacify but also of something to be pacified. In this instance it is the recognition of evil. "The devil must have his due," we say. Here the "beast" must be mollified, given its due. Jack recognizes this fact, even if he and his group of hunters do not understand it. Politically and anthropologically he is more instinctive than Ralph. Jack does not symbolize chaos, as sometimes claimed, but, rather, a stronger, more primitive order than Ralph provides.

Jack's chief henchman, Roger, is not so subtly or complexly characterized, and seems to belong more to Orwellian political fable. Slightly younger and physically weaker, he possesses from the beginning all the sadistic attributes of the demagogue's hangman underling. In his treatment of the sow he proves deserving of his appellation in English slang. Through his intense, furtive, silent qualities, he acts as a sinister foil to Simon. By the end of the novel Golding has revealed Roger; we hardly need to be told that "the hangman's horror clung round him."

Simon is perhaps the most effectively—and certainly the most poignantly—characterized of all. A "skinny, vivid little boy, with a glance coming up from under a hut of straight hair that hung down, black and coarse," he is (at nine or ten) the lonely visionary, the clear-sighted realist, logical, sensitive, and mature beyond his years. We learn that he has a history of epileptic seizures—a dubious endowment sometimes credited to great men of the past, particularly those with a touch of the mystic. We see the unusual grace and sensitivity of his personality crop up here and there as the story unfolds until he becomes the central figure of the "Lord of the Flies" scene—one of Golding's most powerful and poetic. We see Simon's instinctive compassion and intelligence as he approaches the rotting corpse of the parachutist, which, imprisoned in the rocks on the hill in flying suit and parachute harness, is the only palpable "monster" on the island. Although Simon's senses force him to vomit with revulsion, he nevertheless frees it "from the wind's indignity." When he returns to tell his frightened, blood-crazed companions that, in effect, they have nothing to fear but fear itself, his murder becomes the martyrdom of a saint and prophet, a point in human degeneration next to which the wanton killing of Piggy is but an anticlimax. In some of the novel's richest, most sensitive prose, the body of Simon (the boys' "beast" from the jungle) is taken out to sea by the tide, Golding here reaching close to tragic exaltation as Simon is literally transfigured in death. . . .

With his mysterious touch of greatness Simon comes closest to foreshadowing the kind of hero Golding himself has seen as representing man's greatest need if he is to advance in his humanity—the Saint Augustines, Shakespeares, and Mozarts, "inexplicable, miraculous." Piggy, on the other hand, who, just before his own violent death, clutches at a rationalization for Simon's murder, has all the good and bad attributes of the weaker sort of intellectual. Despised by Jack and protected by Ralph, he is set off from the others by his spectacles, asthma, accent, and very fat, short body. Freudian analysts would have Piggy stand as superego, but he is extremely id-directed toward food: it is Ralph who must try to hold him back from accepting Jack's pig meat, and Ralph who acts as strong conscience in making Piggy accept partial responsibility for Simon's death. Although ranked as one of the "biguns," Piggy is physically incapable and emotionally immature. The logic of his mind is insufficient to cope with the human problems of their coral-island situation. But this insight into him is fictionally denied to the Ralphs of this world, who (as on the last page of the novel) weep not for Simon, but for "the true, wise friend called Piggy." . . .

. . . In the years of exegesis since publication of *Lord of the Flies*, critical analysis has been hardening into dogmatic opinion, much of it allegoristic, as evidenced by such titles as "Allegories of Innocence," "Secret Parables," and "The Fables of William Golding." And even where the titles are not indicative (as with E. L. Epstein's Capricorn edition afterword, and the equally Freudian analysis of Claire Rosenfield), critical literature has generally forced the book into a neat allegorical novel. The temptation is strong, since the novel is evocative and the characters seem to beg for placement within handy categories of meaning—political, sociological, religious, and psychological categories. Yet Golding is a simply complicated writer; and, so much the better for the novel as novel, none of the boxes fits precisely.

Oversimplifying, Frederick Karl writes that "When the boys on the island struggle for supremacy, they re-enact a ritual of the adult world, as much as the college Fellows in Snow's *The Masters* work out the ritual of a power struggle in the larger world." Jack may appear to be the demagogic dictator and Roger his sadistic henchman; Ralph may be a confused democrat, with Piggy his "brain trust"; but the neatness of the political allegory is complicated by the clear importance of the mystical, generalization-defying Simon. Although Simon, who alone among the boys has gone up to the mountaintop and discovered the truth, is sacrificed in a subhuman orgy, those who have seen a religious allegory in the novel find it more in the fall of man from paradise, as the island Eden turns into a fiery hell, and the Satanic Jack into the fallen archangel. But Ralph makes only a tenuous Adam; the sow is a sorry Eve; and Piggy, the sightless sage, has no comfortable place in Christian myth. Further, it is an ironic commentary upon religious interpretations of *Lord of the Flies* that of an island full of choirboys, not one ever resorts—even automatically—to prayer or to appeals to a deity, not even before they begin backsliding. And the Edenic quality of the island paradise is compromised from the beginning, for, although the essentials of life are abundant, so are the essentials of pain, terror, and death: the fruit which makes them ill, the animals which awaken their bloodthirstiness and greed, the cruel war in the air above them, the darkness and the unknown which beget their fears.

As a social allegory of human regression the novel is more easily (perhaps too neatly) explainable as "the way in which, when the civilized restraints which we impose on ourselves are abandoned, the passions of anger, lust and fear wash across the mind, obliterating commonsense and care, and life once again becomes nasty, brutish and short." The island itself is shaped like a boat, and takes on symbolic proportions, not simply in the microcosmic-macrocosmic sense, but as subtle foreshadowing of the regression about to take place among the boys: "It was roughly boat-shaped. . . . The tide was running so that long streaks of foam tailed away from the reef and for a moment they felt that the boat was moving steadily astern." This sternward movement not only conjures up the regressive backsliding away from civilization that constitutes the theme of the novel, but is imagistically associated with Piggy's "ass-mar" and the general note of scatology—as with the littluns being "taken short" in the orchard—which prevails in this book on Beelzebub, lord of the flies *and* dung. Later, when Simon asks the assembly to think of the dirtiest thing imaginable, Jack answers with the monosyllable for excrement. This is not what Simon means at all: he is thinking of the evil in man. But the two concepts merge in Golding's imagination. . . .

Some critics who see the allegory of evil as just the surface meaning of the novel have been led into psychological labyrinths, where Jack appears as the Freudian id personified; Ralph the ego; and Piggy the superego, conscience of the grown-up world. But William Wasserstrom has dealt severely with Miss Rosenfield in this kind of interpretation; the experts have fallen out; and, besides, the Freudian *ménage à trois* fails to accommodate the vital Simon. Indeed, the problem in all attempts to explain *Lord of the Flies* as some kind of parable is that the novel is not a parable: it is too long, and lacks the point-by-point parallelism necessary to meet the definition. Nor, in the precise sense, is it a fable, since it deals primarily with human beings, since it does not rely upon folkloristic or fantastic materials, and since it does not provide the convenience of an explicit moral. It *is* allegoristic, rich in variant suggestions, and best taken at the level of suggestive analysis.

This novel has been taken, too, as a straight tale of initiation, with Ralph as hero—an interpretation to which the book's ending is particularly susceptible. Yet there is more to it than Ralph's facing a brutal adult world with a lament for his lost childhood and for the innocence he thinks has been stripped from him. What Ralph dimly fathoms, the naval-officer "rescuer" cannot possibly understand—that the world, in the words of Shaw's Saint Joan, is not yet ready to receive its saints, neither its Simons nor even its Piggys and Ralphs. Whether he means it or not Golding provides a hopeful note, for even at mankind's present stage of development Piggy and Ralph, the latter with shame, relapse only slightly toward the barbarism of their contemporaries (and that of the officer, who is engaged in a no less barbaric war "outside"); while Simon withstands the powerful regressive pressures completely. That these three represent three-quarters of the novel's major characters defeats any explanation of the novel in totally pessimistic terms.

Almost endlessly, the four major characters are thematically suggestive, and are usually identified in the book with certain imagery and talismanic objects: Jack with blood and dung, with the mask of primitive tribalism (imagistically he is in league with the Lord of the Flies); Piggy with pigs' meat (his physical sloth and appetite and eventual sacrifice), with his glasses, which represent intellect and science (though they could hardly coax the sun into making fire); Ralph with the conch and signal fire, with comeliness and the call to duty, with communal hope (all shattered when the conch dwindles in power and is finally shattered, and the signal fire dies out). Again, however, it may be Simon—not so thematically suggestive as the others—who provides the best clues to . . . Golding's intentions, for we recall not only his mysticism, his intelligence, his fragility, but also his association with the bees and butterflies that hover sweetly and innocently (by comparison with the flies) about the island, and the tragic beauty of his transfiguration. Perhaps it is Simon who best suggests Golding's optimism in the face of his apparent allegory of regression. "The human spirit," writes Golding, "is wider and more complex than the whole of the physical evolutionary system. . . . We shall have . . . to conform more and more closely to categories or go under. But the change in politics, in religion, in art, in literature will come, because it *will* come; because the human spirit is limitless and inexhaustible." Just around the corner, he promises, are the Saint Augustines, Shakespeares, and Mozarts: "Perhaps they are growing up now."

What can be said of *Lord of the Flies* eventually is that, in structure and narrative method, it is Golding's simplest novel. . . . But it is not an obvious novel, as sometimes claimed. It shares with his other books an ending technique that constitutes a reversal—a sudden shift of viewpoint. Here the timely arrival of the naval officer acts as no concession to readers demanding a happy ending. What we get instead of "gimmick" or conventional *deus ex machina* is a necessary change of focus: the boys, who have grown almost titanic in their struggle, are suddenly seen again as boys, some merely tots, dirty-nosed and bedraggled. And then a retrospective irony results, since the boys deserve to be thought of as titanic: if they have been fighting our battle, we realize—with both hope and dismay—that mankind is still in something of a prepuberty stage. Thus *Lord of the Flies* ends as no act of hope or charity or even contrition. It is an act of recognition.

The tone is peculiarly calm: Golding keeps his distance from his materials; he does not interfere or preach; and the material is made to speak for itself through a simplicity of prose style and a naturalistic-allegorical form. The vision of Golding is through both ends of the telescope. . . .

In Recognizing Their Savage Nature, Humans Gain Maturity

Minnie Singh

Minnie Singh is a literary critic.

In the following essay, Minnie Singh calls Lord of the Flies *a parody of R.M. Ballantyne's* The Coral Island. *Golding takes the island paradise and innocent characters of the earlier work and replaces them with an island that becomes a deadly, infernal place and with children who become savages. Singh contends that Golding's message is that savagery lurks under the surface of civilization. Singh argues, however, that if one recognizes one's essential savagery, one has the potential to conquer it and mature as a person.*

A memorable scene early in William Golding's 1954 *Lord of the Flies* eloquently suggests the ambition of Golding's fabulist intentions. On the island that at this point in the text is still an innocent playground, one of the younger boys, Henry, who is building castles in the sand, is covertly observed by an older boy, Roger:

> Roger stooped, picked up a stone, aimed, and threw it at Henry—threw it to miss. The stone—that token of preposterous time—bounced five yards to the right and fell in the water. Roger gathered a handful of stones and began to throw them. Yet there was a space round Henry, perhaps six yards in diameter, into which he dared not throw. Here, invisible yet strong, was the taboo of the old life. Round the squatting child was the protection of parents and school and

Minnie Singh, "The Government of Boys: Golding's *Lord of the Flies* and Ballantyne's *Coral Island*," *Children's Literature*, vol. 25, 1997, pp. 205–13. Copyright © 1997 The Johns Hopkins University Press. Reproduced by permission.

policemen and the law. Roger's arm was conditioned by a civilization that knew nothing of him and was in ruins.

The "space round Henry, perhaps six yards in diameter," into which Roger dare not throw, is nothing other than the shrunken dimensions of civil society—the restraints taught by parents, school, policemen, and the law. What Roger is unable to disobey is not the express prohibition of civil society against violence, but an internalized restraint—that is, civility. Significantly, in the penultimate chapter of the book, it is Roger who hurls the mighty rock that sends Piggy crashing to his death: more starkly than any other character, he represents the erosion of restraint, the return to a sort of Stone Age. If the project of government may be understood macropolitically as civilization, then its micropolitical counterpart is education, with civility as its project. Golding's text is notable for making explicit this cluster of associations, which has long been the implicit staple of the literature of boyhood.

A Parody of *The Coral Island*

Lord of the Flies is an overseas adventure story, the self-conscious culmination of a long line of boys' adventure stories. "It's like in a book," Ralph announces after their initial exploration of the island:

> At once there was a clamour.
>
> "Treasure Island—"
>
> "Swallows and Amazons—"
>
> "Coral Island—"
>
> . . . .
>
> "This is our island. It's a good island. Until the grownups come to fetch us we'll have fun."

Golding's story seeks to dispel this intertextual glamor with grim realism; it both participates in and criticizes the history of the adventure story, whose originating canonical text is *Robinson Crusoe*. But the adventure story that was almost schematically Golding's pre-text was Robert Michael Ballantyne's 1858 *Coral Island*, one of the earliest such stories to have boys, in the absence of adults, for its main characters. . . .

More than a century after Ballantyne's daring and successful experiment in boys literature, William Golding declared, in his 1962 lecture at Berkeley on the writing of *Lord of the Flies*: "Ballantyne's island was a nineteenth-century island inhabited by English boys; mine was to be a twentieth-century island inhabited by English boys." Written out of the agonized consciousness of England's loss of global power, *Lord of the Flies* may be read with some accuracy as a parodic rewriting of Ballantyne's *Coral Island*. The three central characters of *Lord of the Flies*—Ralph, Piggy, and Jack—are caricatures of Ballantyne's three boy heroes—Ralph, Peterkin, and Jack—who, shipwrecked on an island like Crusoe's (albeit in the South Seas), heroically survive violent encounters with cannibalistic natives and bloodthirsty pirates. The idyllic Coral Island is transformed by Golding into an infernal place: whereas Ballantyne's adventurers master nature, using and developing technology for the purpose, Golding's boy characters are helpless captives whose only hope is rescue. . . .

Both Novels Are Concerned with Savagery

[*Lord of the Flies* and *The Coral Island*] are overwhelmingly similar in their thematic concern with legitimate authority, leadership, and government. Both texts equate good government with the containment and defeat of savagery (whether the savagery is shown to reside within us or without); and both characterize savagery as the absence of a restraining law. Late in *The Coral Island*, the narrator, Ralph, who is now separated from his comrades, appeals to the pirate Bill, his guide through the South Sea islands:

Scene from the 1963 film adaptation of William Golding's Lord of the Flies. *Two Arts/CD/The Kobal Collection/The Picture Desk, Inc.*

"Have these wretched creatures [native islanders] no law among themselves," said I, "which can restrain such wickedness?"

"None," replied Bill. "The chief's word is law. He might kill and eat a dozen of his own subjects any day for nothing more than his own pleasure, and nobody would take the least notice of it."

A cluster of associations equates the pirates with "white savages" and their savagery, like that of the natives, manifests itself in "wanton slaughter." If the restraint of pleasure is the defining characteristic of civilization, then boyhood, Ballantyne appears to suggest, is that state of grace where pleasure is harmless, appetite is healthy, and play is productive. Beyond boyhood, pleasure must be restrained, appetite curbed, and play governed.

Lord of the Flies proposes its own version of irresponsible authority in the terrifying figure of Jack, who "makes things break up like they do." The Jack of *The Coral Island* had been a natural leader who ruled by superior knowledge—he had read more adventure stories than had the others—and by playful violence. Golding's Jack, on the other hand, is clearly drawn from contemporary alarms about the totalitarian personality. It must be remembered that *Lord of the Flies* achieves its ominous generality of reference by glossing over the specificity of its Cold War context. The boys suspect that there has been a nuclear explosion, and, at the end, Ralph's greatest remembered fear is of the "Reds." Golding himself uses the term "totalitarian"—a word that only took on its full negative import after World War II—in his remarks on *Lord of the Flies*:

> Before the Second World War I believed in the perfectibility of social man; that a correct structure of society would produce goodwill; and that therefore you could remove all social ills by a reorganization of society. It is possible that today I believe something of the same, but after the war I did not because I was unable to. I had discovered what one man could do to another. . . . I am thinking of the vileness beyond all words that went on, year after year, in the totalitarian states . . . there were things done during that period from which I still have to avert my mind lest I should be physically sick. They were not done by the head-hunters of New Guinea, or by some primitive tribe in the Amazon. They were done skilfully, coldly, by educated men, doctors, lawyers, by men with a tradition of civilization behind them, to beings of their own kind.

Golding finally leaves us with the not entirely convincing position that totalitarianism is a form of savagery, and that not even boyhood is exempt from its encroachments. In Golding's own formulation,

> Man is a fallen being. He is gripped by original sin. His nature is sinful and his state perilous. . . . I looked round me

for some convenient form in which this thesis might be worked out, and found it in the play of children. I was well situated for this, since at this time I was teaching them. Moreover, I am a son, brother, father. I have lived for many years with small boys, and understand and know them with awful precision. I decided to take the literary convention of boys on an island, only make them real boys instead of paper cutouts with no life in them; and try to show how the shape of the society they evolved would be conditioned by their diseased, their fallen nature.

Savagery at the Heart of Civilization

Rhetorically and ideologically, the claim of *Lord of the Flies* over *The Coral Island* is the claim of experience over innocence, realism over romance, truth over illusion, maturity over naivete, and hardship over ease. At a crucial narrative moment in *Lord of the Flies*, before the reversion to savagery is properly under way, Ralph, the good leader, has an introspective realization: "He found himself understanding the weariness of this life, where every path was an improvisation and a considerable part of one's waking life was spent watching one's feet. He stopped, facing the strip; and remembering that first enthusiastic exploration as though it were part of a brighter childhood, he smiled jeeringly." *Lord of the Flies* encourages us to locate the possibility of good government in the irrecoverable brighter childhood of political thought. At the same time, it makes childhood itself as archaic as the colonial metaphor of enthusiastic exploration. . . .

Lord of the Flies takes considerable pains to establish that at the heart of civilization lurks a persistent savagery, and that men, once stripped of the veneer of adulthood, quickly revert to being wanton boys who kill one another for their sport. Indeed, the book's remarkable success has made the reversion to savagery a cultural byword, and a powerful one because it represents the transformation from the civilized to the savage as simultaneously regression and maturation. To become savage is to regress to the anthropological infancy of mankind, but to recognize one's essential savagery is to be psychologically mature: this is the intriguingly mixed message of Golding's book.

Lord of the Flies Is a Political, Psychological, and Religious Allegory

Diane Andrews Henningfeld

Diane Andrews Henningfeld was a professor at Adrian College in Michigan from 1987 to 2008.

In the following essay Diane Andrews Henningfeld finds Lord of the Flies *to be an allegory on three levels: political, Freudian, and Christian. Politically, each of four major characters—Ralph, Jack, Roger, and Piggy—represents a type of government. A Freudian reading has Ralph representing the ego, Jack the id, and Piggy the superego. As a religious allegory, the island can be seen as an Eden, and the story becomes the story of the Fall of Man. Henningfeld contends the novel works both as a compelling adventure story and an allegory.*

*L*ord of the Flies is deliberately modeled after R. M. Ballantyne's 1857 novel *The Coral Island*. In this story, a group of English boys are shipwrecked on a tropical island. They work hard together to save themselves. The only evil in the book is external and is personified by a tribe of cannibals that live on the island. The book offers a Victorian view of the world: through hard work and earnestness, one can overcome any hardship.

By giving his characters the same names as those in Ballantyne's book and by making direct reference to *The Coral Island* in the text of *Lord of the Flies*, Golding clearly wants readers to see his book as a response to the Victorian world view. Golding's view is a much bleaker one: the evil on the is-

Diane Andrews Henningfeld, "An Overview of *Lord of the Flies,*" *Exploring Novels*; reprinted in *Literature Resource Center*, December 27, 2008. Reproduced by permission of Gale, a part of Cengage Learning.

land is internal, not external. At the end of the book, the adult naval officer who invokes *The Coral Island* almost serves as Ballantyne's voice: "I should have thought that a pack of British boys—you're all British, aren't you?—would have been able to put up a better show than that." Golding's understanding of the world, colored by his own experiences in World War II, is better represented by Ralph's weeping "for the end of innocence, the darkness of man's heart, and the fall through the air of the true, wise friend called Piggy." . . .

Many critics have argued that *Lord of the Flies* is an allegory. An allegory is a story in which characters, setting, objects, and plot stand for a meaning outside of the story itself. Frequently, the writers of allegory illustrate an abstract meaning by the use of concrete images. . . . Often, characters in allegories personify some abstract quality. . . .

While it is possible to read *Lord of the Flies* as allegory, the work is so complex that it can be read as allegorizing the political state of the world in the postwar period; as a Freudian psychological understanding of humankind; or as the Christian understanding of the fall of humankind, among others.

A Political Allegory

As a political allegory, each character in *Lord of the Flies* represents some abstract idea of government. Ralph, for example, stands for the good-hearted but not entirely effective leader of a democratic state, a ruler who wants to rule by law derived from the common consent. Piggy is his adviser, someone who is unable to rule because of his own social and physical shortcomings, but who is able to offer sound advice to the democratic leader. Jack, on the other hand, represents a totalitarian dictator, a ruler who appeals to the emotional responses of his followers. He rules by charisma and hysteria. Roger, the boy who takes the most joy in the slaughter of the pigs and who hurls the rock that kills Piggy, represents the henchman necessary for such a totalitarian ruler to stay in power.

Such a reading takes into account the state of the world at the end of the World War II. For many years, leaders such as British Prime Minister Winston Churchill and U.S. President Franklin D. Roosevelt led democratic countries against totalitarian demigods such as Germany's Adolf Hitler and Italy's Benito Mussolini. Further, in the early 1950s, the world appeared to be divided into two camps: the so-called Free World of Western Europe and the United States, and the so-called Iron Curtain world of communist eastern Europe and the Soviet Union. At the time of the writing of *Lord of the Flies*, the world appeared to be teetering on the brink of total nuclear annihilation. Thus, by taking into account the historical context of *Lord of the Flies*, it is possible to understand the work as political and historical allegory, even as a cautionary tale for the leaders of the world.

A Psychological Allegory

Freudian psychological critics, on the other hand, are able to read *Lord of the Flies* as an allegory of the human psychology. In such a reading, each of the characters personifies a different aspect of the human psyche: the id, the super ego, and the ego. According to Freud, the id (located in the unconscious mind) works always to gratify its own impulses. These impulses, often sexual, seek to provide pleasure without regard to the cost. Jack's impulse to hunt and kill reaches its peak with the killing of the sow pig, a killing rife with sexual overtones. Jack never considers anything but his own pleasure; thus he can be considered an allegorical representation of the id. The superego is the part of the mind that seeks to control the impulsive behavior of the id. It acts as an internal censor. In *Lord of the Flies*, Piggy serves this role. He constantly reminds Ralph of their need to keep the fire burning and to take proper responsibility for the littluns. By so doing, he urges Ralph to control Jack. Piggy understands that Jack hates him, because he stands between Jack and his achievement of pleasure. Further, just as the superego must employ the ego to control the id, Piggy cannot control Jack on his own; he must rely on Ralph to do so. Finally, the ego is the conscious mind whose role it is to mediate between the id's demand for pleasure and the social pressures brought to bear by the superego. Freud calls this mediation process the reality principle; that is, the notion that immediate pleasure must be denied in order to avoid painful or deadly consequences. Ralph clearly fills this role. He attempts to control Jack and engage his energy for the tending of the fire. To do so requires him to put off the pleasure of the hunt in order to secure rescue. In a Freudian reading of *Lord of the Flies*, Golding seems to be saying that without the reinforcement of social norms, the id will control the psyche.

A Religious Allegory

Finally, it is possible to read *Lord of the Flies* as a religious allegory. In such a reading, the tropical island, filled with fruit and everything needed for sustenance, becomes a symbol of the Garden of Eden. The initial identification of the beastie as a snake also brings to mind the story of the Fall of Man. Indeed, it is possible to read the fall of the parachutist as the event which leads to the ouster from Eden of the boys. Further, Jack's identification with hunting and Ralph's identification with shelter as well as their natural antagonism appear to be allegorization of the Cain and Abel story. Indeed, it is only the intercession of the adult who comes looking for them which saves Ralph from murder. Many critics have attempted to read Simon as a Christ figure; he is the one boy who has the true knowledge which can save them. Like Christ, he is martyred. Unlike Christ, however, his death seems to have no significance for the boys; his knowledge dies with him. . . .

Golding also provides strong characterizations. While it is possible to see each boy fulfilling an allegorical role, none of the characters (with the possible exception of Simon) functions solely as part of the allegory. This can perhaps best be seen in the development of Jack. During the first trip into the jungle, he is unable to kill the pig with his knife; by the end of the book he is hunting human quarry. Jack's growth from choirboy to murderer is accomplished with great skill.

Finally, Golding writes a fast-moving, suspenseful adventure story. The book moves quickly from the first days on the beach to the final hunt scene, reaching a feverish pitch that is broken abruptly by the appearance of the naval officer, just as it appears that Ralph will be killed. While the appearance of the adult, however, closes the action, it does not provide us with a happy ending. Indeed, at the moment of the climax of the adventure story, Golding suddenly reminds us of the allegorical nature of the book: the naval officer's cruiser is a weapon of war. Although we feel relief over Ralph's rescue, we suddenly understand that the adult world is little different from the world of the island, a place where men hunt and kill each other indiscriminately, a place where men can blow up the entire planet, our island in the sea of the universe.

The Violence in *Lord of the Flies* Results from the Failure to Accept Responsibility

Kenneth Watson

Kenneth Watson was a senior lecturer in English at Stranmillis College in Belfast, Northern Ireland.

In this viewpoint, Kenneth Watson calls Lord of the Flies *a social and political fable. He suggests that the four main characters represent different aspects of society. Ralph is the flawed liberal politician; Jack, the authoritarian despot; Piggy, the scientist; and Simon, the rationalist who combines both intellectual and emotional wisdom. The source of the evil that overtakes the island is not from original sin, Watson argues, but from a failure of imagination that prevents the boys from cooperating with each other.*

The clearest tribute I know to the power and realism of *Lord of the Flies* is the shock of its impact on even non-literary students, precisely because it is not 'literary' but unfalteringly tough-minded. Its first reading is for most people a frightening experience, arousing a sense of uncanny and even supernatural evil like that which almost—but never quite—engulfs Simon. This subjective but common experience is a relevant critical reaction in distinguishing the quality of the novel, if it is consolidated by objective analysis. The immediacy of the writing is at once apparent in the imagery, with metaphors often embedded in the verbs, in the observant eye firmly on the object, and in an at times poetic transforming imagination:

> 'The eye was first attracted to a black bat-like creature that danced on the sand, and only later perceived the body above

Kenneth Watson, "A Reading of *Lord of the Flies*," *English*, vol. 15, no. 85, Spring 1964, pp. 2–7. Copyright © The English Association 1964. Reproduced by permission.

it. The bat was the child's shadow, shrunk by the vertical sun to a patch between the hurrying feet.

'This sweaty march along the blazing beach had given them the complexion of newly washed plums.'

Terrifying Spiritual Claustrophobia

The tropical detail combines with an occasional reminder of its effects on the boys to give an awareness of their physical plight. Even the sea plays surprisingly little part in their lives and the reef is completely inaccessible. The only escape from the confines of the island and the march of events is Ralph's remembrance of having once lived in a Devon cottage on the edge of the moors.

Even more important than this restriction to the island is the entire absence of adults. This, together with a refusal ever to release the reader by intruding with personal comment, produces an utterly claustrophobic effect, spiritual as much as physical. It is this spiritual claustrophobia which makes the hunting of Ralph so terrifying, so that one experiences such a sudden shock of contrast when the mob of merciless and howling savages suddenly shoots down to child size and Jack becomes smaller than he appeared in the opening pages: 'a little boy who wore the remains of an extraordinary black cap on his red hair', in contrast to the 'huge peaked cap' of the naval officer.

Both the sensory accuracy and the emotional concentration are essential foundations for the reader's fuller experience of the work. As in *The Ancient Mariner* they give firmness and clarity to the symbolism, which arises directly from character and event. Mr. Golding's novels are usually called fables; it is this exactness in both action and description (the description is never static or separate from event) which supports us in experiencing and therefore accepting the moral fable.

A Moral Message

Obviously the progress of the plot can be compared to the Fall [of man]. But once any tendency, especially towards chaos or lawlessness, establishes itself, it progresses at ever-growing speed towards its climax. Any accomplished writer would give increasing pace to the narrative through the need for increasing tension. Nor is the plot in the form of a single unbroken movement: the episode which is both the most important and the most moving, though not the most purely terrifying, is the death of Simon. Is there perhaps a use for Occam's Razor [philosophical principle holding that the simplest answer is usually the correct one] in the theological interpretation of *Lord of the Flies*? To take it as symbolizing the Fall may be a valid personal interpretation, but I do not find it a necessary one—though this is not of course to exclude interpretation in terms of religious *ethic*. But 'the darkness of man's heart', deterioration into fear and cruelty, do not necessitate a reading based on 'original sin'. To say so is no more valid today than is the old free-will and determinism antithesis. And if the island is the paradise within which the 'Fall' occurs, it is so only in a very limited sense of unrestricted fruit, warmth, and enervation. It is far from an ideal environment even physically. The fruit is an inadequate diet which produces diarrhoea, the littluns exist in squalor and neglect, and it is problems of discomfort and trying to organize obvious needs, such as the fire, and shelter from both rain and fear, which soon cause the first splits and outbursts of ill feeling.

But the deeper levels of meaning can, I think, be identified more precisely. The novel works most vitally in moral, not religious or theological, terms. Ralph has even been described as a father figure who represents virtue and light. But he is too clearly flawed. The beginning of cruelty, unthinking as always, must be important in a work so tightly constructed as this. And it comes from Ralph, and is doubly significant because he is the only character through whose eyes and feelings we perceive directly at times and with whom we, to some degree, identify ourselves. The initial cruelty is the betrayal of Piggy's nickname; his real name is never known because Ralph never troubles to ask it. As for light, it is Piggy and later Simon who hold up the torch. They alone resist the growth of superstition; Piggy through rational thought, Simon by the strength of his own conviction, which unlike the intellectual literal-mindedness of Piggy grows under the stress put upon it. He has faith: but in what? By holding fast to the power of his own mind he interprets the evidence of his senses in the light of what he knows.

A Social and Political Fable

There is evidently not only a moral and intellectual fable but a social and political one. Ralph is *l'homme moyen sensuel* [Everyman] but even more clearly the 'liberal' politician who has found he can talk fluently and enjoys the applause of the crowd.

'The assembly was silent.

'Ralph lifted the conch again and his good humour came back as he thought of what he had to say next.

'"Now we come to the most important thing. I've been thinking. I was thinking while we were climbing the mountain." He flashed a conspiratorial grin at the other two. "And on the beach just now. This is what I thought. We want to have fun. And we want to be rescued."'

This is an epitome of the political oratory, based on emotion but nothing else, which carries the speaker along with it as much as the hearers.

'The passionate noise of agreement from the assembly hit him like a wave and he lost his thread. He thought again.

'"We want to be rescued; and of course we shall be rescued."

'Voices babbled. The simple statement, unbacked by any proof but the weight of Ralph's new authority, brought light and happiness.'

This cannot be satisfactorily read on the narrative level alone: the parallels are too close and insistent. His words induce simple euphoria; 'important', 'thinking', and especially 'light' are ironic and the happiness is without foundation or possibility of endurance. This represents the quality of his mind in contrast to Piggy's while also implying its common quality with his audience's. Later, in another mood 'he found himself understanding the wearisomeness of this life where every path was an improvisation and a considerable part of one's waking life was spent watching one's feet'.

'The time had come for the assembly, and as he walked into the concealing splendours of the sunlight he went carefully over the points of his speech. There must be no mistake about this assembly, no chasing imaginary . . .

'He lost himself in a maze of thoughts that were rendered vague by his lack of words to express them. Frowning, he tried again.

'This meeting must not be fun, but business.'

Piggy Is Lower Class and Sees the Truth

It is enlightening to read the accounts of the four assemblies successively and notice how increasingly, as the shutter comes down and the curtain flaps in his well-intentioned mind, Ralph has to be prompted by Piggy to save him from completely losing his grip on the clue of the actual.

The most explicit symbol is the conch. Since it carries the right to be heard, the mandate to speak even for a littlun if he holds it, it implies that the rule of law still exists. Jack, who epitomizes the course of political change followed by most authoritarian demagogues, is the first to demand rules for his own advantage, but the first to shout them down later. When the conch is smashed—it and Piggy, the rational non-violent person, are wiped out at the same moment and by the same blow, for Piggy's separateness leaves him no other protection—then all attempt to maintain social order is ended and barbarism is loose. Piggy has been established at once as a realist: while Ralph stands on his head at the thought of no grown-ups, Piggy says the plane will not be back—and why. Ralph's belated recognition of him—forging a link which till then had been with Jack—comes because Piggy shows he can think: see essentials, criticize, and make suggestions. He is interested in the life of the rock pool and knows about mirages, in strong contrast to Ralph's casual mind, with its continual daydreams. It is Piggy who first says they must have a meeting, and he is the organizer who tries to collect names—and at this stage is obeyed. Indeed only the myopic Piggy is clear-sighted enough to see what their problems and needs actually are and how they are failing more and more to meet them. 'Like a crowd of kids', he says repeatedly. His is the particular agony of the mature in mind.

> 'We could experiment. We could find out how to make a small hot fire and then put green branches on to make smoke. Some of them leaves must be better for that than others.'

This is the scientific attitude, the intellectual emancipation that applies empirical thought and experiment to any new problem, making comparisons and establishing priorities and values, even in changed circumstances. 'Only Piggy could have the intellectual daring to suggest moving the fire from the mountain.' In ironic contrast to his physical timidity and social ineffectiveness is his intellectual courage in facing facts even when horrified by them, about people as well as things. His imagination tells him why Jack hates him, and he realizes earlier than Ralph that Jack and Roger have gone to set up their own gang. While the rest want reassurance, not truth, he

Scene from the 1963 film adaptation of William Golding's Lord of the Flies. *Two Arts/ CD/The Kobal Collection/The Picture Desk, Inc.*

says: 'How can you expect to be rescued if you don't put first things first and act proper?' Finally, in a book where every close-packed detail has significance, there should be meaning in the fact that he is the only boy who does not come from a conventional middle-class background.... Helpless in the absence of protection, he seems to stand as the representative social democrat and intellectual, over against both the conventional member of the 'officer class' presumed to have automatic powers of 'leadership' and those who take ease and affluence for granted.

The Unknown Citizen

Social attitudes and types are plain behind the remarkable individualization of the boys. Characters emerge. They do not change, but traits grow as changing circumstances feed them. Irony plays most on Ralph and Jack. What they have in common is vanity, but where there is a 'mildness' about Ralph, Jack's eyes are frustrated and ready to turn to anger at our first sight of him. He and his hunters are already uniformed, and Piggy, intimidated, asks no names. Jack, oblivious of other needs, scorns all who do not hunt as he does, and his joke 'Use a littlun' for the pig in the ritual dance is not quite a joke. His mortification when not in the full limelight and his lust to hunt and kill, rationalized as providing meat, feed each other till he is swallowed by his own mad unreal world in which everything is transformed with the ingenuity of the paranoiac to fit his fantasy, and Simon's body becomes the beast—disguised. In the completest possible contrast to Piggy he says, 'Forget the beast and sacrifice to it.'

The others do, sooner or later. Samneric, their identities lost not just because they are twins, become in the face of power the ordinary good-hearted nonentities most of us are, who protest at first and remain loyal, then defect under increasing, and finally physical, pressure, but retain their humane impulses and will take risks at times, as in warning Ralph. Roger's essential nature is shown early:

> 'Roger led the way straight through the castles, kicking them over, burying the flowers, scattering the chosen stones.'

'A slight furtive boy whom no one knew', he finds the beginnings of ecstasy in the stone-throwing, and becomes the eager executioner of the cruelties decreed by the Leader who does not need to carry them out himself. 'The hangman's horror clung around him' as he brusquely corrects the chief's crude, inefficient attempt to torture Sam:

> '"That's not the way."

> 'Roger edged past the chief, only just avoiding pushing him with his shoulder. The yelling ceased and Samneric lay looking up in quiet terror.'

One knows from this why the concentration camps could always be staffed, as through Jack's 'numberless and inexpressible frustrations' one has an insight into the psychology of a Hitler.

And the littlun with the birthmark, who disappears in the fire, leaving no trace and remembered only by Piggy (he was never even noticed till he resisted notice): does he not represent the anonymous millions, the Unknown Citizen who has existed throughout history and before it, and still exists till obliterated by forces, part human, part natural, which he can neither control nor even understand? It is remarkable that at the end when the naval officer, 'who knew as a rule when people were telling the truth', asks if anyone has been killed, Ralph's answer is 'Only two'. The point is that this is truthful as far as he or anyone else is aware. The memory of the very existence of a littlun (the word is always written as a common noun) has been repressed, as presence at the murder of Simon becomes taboo even to Piggy. I have been more than once struck by the fact that in reading *Lord of the Flies*, many students, not usually careless readers, accept at first Ralph's statement and themselves forget the third death, simply because, I think, their minds work like most people's.

A Failure of Imagination

But all this is moral, psychological, social; not theological. While the spreading evil emanates from the boys themselves, they deteriorate not under any inner compulsion of original sin, but through a failure of imagination and therefore a neglect of thought, which leads them to ignore their own opportunities and the plight of others alike, so that they refuse to co-operate even for their own advantage. That is to say, they are a microcosm of the adult world; incomplete, but one which, since it excludes all manifestations of sex, which is essentially individual, emphasizes still more powerfully the elements of society. This is the world of which Piggy and Ralph say pathetically that grown-ups would not quarrel or talk about a beast, and their belief may represent the unwisdom of relying on the unaided intellect. The ironic comment on it is the uncomprehending naval officer's cliché: 'I should have thought that a pack of British boys—you're all British, aren't you?—would have been able to put up a better show than that', which is no better than Jack's rabid nationalism: 'After all, we're not savages. We're English; and the English are best at everything.' Above all, in their frenzy the boys are unable even to hear the truth, that is, the plain facts, that Simon brings them from the hill. Cruelty has crept in as always in intrinsically small ways, through imaginative laziness and failure of sympathy, till callousness hardens more and more. Even the killing of the pig, made worse by the emphasis at this point on the beauty of the surroundings, is shown as a brutal act and the animal as needing compassion.

Simon Has Integrity

The hunting of Ralph is the final example of the construction which builds up such emotional intensity by the resonance of incidents repeated with added, or different, significance. The pushing over of the rocks, Roger's repeated stone-throwing, the assemblies, the fires, the hunting scenes, and the dances are merely the more obvious of these 'repetitions with a difference'; there are many smaller ones. The most important is the sight of the 'Beast', first by Samneric, then by Jack and Ralph, and lastly, and with so different a response, by Simon.

Simon is tough-minded, emotionally reliable though physically handicapped; and it is he, not Ralph, who is nobility and light.

"'As if," said Simon, "the beastie, the beastie or the snake-thing, was real. Remember?"

'The two older boys flinched when they heard the shameful syllable. Snakes were not mentioned now, were not mentionable.'

But 'However Simon thought of the beast there arose before his inward sight the picture of a human at once heroic and sick.' Only he stands apart, not simply intellectually like Piggy, but by his very nature; his innate qualities prevent his being smirched like the others. Only he helps Ralph with the shelters; he finds Piggy's glasses and gives him his meat. He volunteers to return across the island alone through the forest. His own weakness makes him pity weakness in others. Like each of those who die, he is set apart by physical defect, but more intensely so. The littlun has 'one side of his face blotted out by a mulberry-coloured birthmark'; Piggy is myopic and asthmatic; Simon is epileptic, and even Piggy says he's cracked. But his strength is that of the martyr he becomes: moral and emotional, a part of him, not an externally sought conviction or faith. He says, 'I think we ought to climb the mountain', and when even Piggy derides this, says: 'What else is there to do?' Having imagination, he is indeed tempted, but never yields. Even when 'one of his times was coming on', 'Simon's mouth laboriously brought forth audible words.'

'Pig's head on a stick'—the gift for the *darkness*. If faith today might be summed up as a belief in explicability together with a belief that everyone is ultimately emotionally educable, then Simon has faith in this sense. Here is the central example in the novel of art as what Joyce Cary called a proposition for truth. In his lonely, half-conscious nightmare he clings to the fact that there is—must be—an explanation, and fights off the inert acceptance of the supernatural. The title marks this as the key, the central scene, and this is not all. Recovering consciousness after his fit, 'Simon spoke aloud to the clearing'.

'What else is there to do?—but keep on. (Piggy at almost this moment is repeating 'We just got to go on, that's all. That's what grownups would do.' But Simon relies on something more integral, less external, than does Piggy.) 'He saw a humped thing suddenly sit up on the top and look down on him.' But 'he hid his face and toiled on.' He not only finds, faces, and understands the 'Beast', 'the mechanics of this parody', which is 'harmless and horrible', but 'he took the lines in his hands, he freed them from the rocks and the figure from the wind's indignity.' There is no supernatural, only the unknown, the not yet understood, the potentially knowable. There is no Beast, either from air or water (for the broken bodies when released are carried out to sea), only ignorance which with fear begets evil in the human imagination and which needs help. So, though 'to speak in assembly was a terrible thing to him', 'the news must reach the others as soon as possible'. Once again 'he felt a perilous necessity to speak', and though once before 'his effort fell about him in ruins; the laughter beat him cruelly', in the moment of death 'Simon was crying out something about a dead man on a hill'. But this is not a clear religious symbol. The dead man on the hill is not Simon who has been tempted in the wilderness and who strives to the death to bring release and salvation from 'mankind's essential illness' to his fellows—through rational understanding.

On the book's first appearance, rather naturally what was first noticed was the parallel with primitive communities. That very original virtuoso performance *The Inheritors* shows the author's interest in the beginnings of the race. But the 're-capitulation theory' is irrelevant here, because, as Mr. Golding has said, he is concerned with the continuing human predicament of living in *this world*, in which modern technology or primitive attempts at weapons or tools are only the attendant circumstances. The world of civilization is a world of savagery still. One of the clearest indications of the social meaning is the war paint and the incantations, reflecting not tribalism so much as the depersonalization, the shedding of identity and therefore of responsibility, which is particularly a modern problem and which is made easy by uniforms, songs, and slogans:

'The mask was a thing on its own, behind which Jack hid, liberated from shame and self-consciousness.'

It is Mr. Golding's conviction that man's destiny is his own responsibility, and man must face this hard fact. . . .

For these are children, immature, undeveloped yet for good or ill. But even more important, there is the non-mystical individual integrity, at once intellectual and emotional, of Simon.

Social Issues in Literature

CHAPTER 3

Contemporary Perspectives on Violence

The War on Terror Is Described as a Battle Between Good and Evil

David R. Mandel

David R. Mandel is a senior scientist at Defence Research and Development Canada and is also an adjunct professor of psychology at the University of Toronto.

In the following viewpoint, David R. Mandel argues that leaders on both sides of the war on terror have enlisted support by characterizing the conflict as a clash between the forces of good and evil. He sees the role of instigator as an important one in unleashing collective violence. Calling for a guerrilla war against Western infidels, Osama bin Laden is the major militant Islamic instigator of terrorism against the West. According to Mandel, former president George W. Bush also vilified the enemy, repeatedly referring to good versus evil when discussing the war against terror. Such categorical thinking, on both sides, can lead to further violence, Mandel contends.

The September 11[, 2001,] terrorist attacks against the United States and the response of the United States and its allies point to the need to critically examine the role of instigators of collective violence. The growing conflict between the United States and its allies and Islamic militant groups has been framed by both sides as a struggle against the forces of evil by the forces of good. These overly simplistic construals of "the other side as evil" and "our side as just" have contributed to an escalation of international violence and threaten us with the possibility of a long-term conflict. In this article, I

David R. Mandel, "Evil and the Instigation of Collective Violence," *Analysis of Social Issues and Public Policy*, vol. 2, no. 1, December 2002, pp. 101–108. Copyright © 2002 The Society for the Psychological Study of Social Issues. Reproduced by permission.

examine the current conflict from a social psychological perspective. I begin by considering the distinction between instigators and perpetrators of collective violence, which has received little scholarly attention until now. I examine briefly how Osama bin Laden, as a key instigator of terrorism over the last decade, has used religious nationalism to rally support for his cause. Finally, I examine how the leaders of both sides—bin Laden and [now former] President George W. Bush—have used the notion of "good versus evil" to frame the present conflict and why such labeling may be effective in rallying support for violent solutions.

Instigators Have Significant Influence

Collective violence is usually described as having three types of agents—perpetrators, victims, and bystanders. Most social psychological research on the topic of evil has tended to focus on how people become socialized into a system of violence and come to function as perpetrators. I have argued recently, however, that a fourth type of agent—the *instigator*—is in dire need of scholarly attention. The function of instigators is not to carry out the acts of violence themselves but to tune and transmit the messages that will effectively motivate others to cause harm and to provide perpetrators with the requisite resources for accomplishing their tasks.

Compared with perpetrators, instigators tend to have greater social influence and a wider range of power. Whereas perpetrators may have access to weaponry or other forms of low-grade power the power of instigators often derives from control of wealth (medium-grade power) and information (high-grade power), which usually provides the requisite conditions for control of weaponry. Indeed, the power that the perpetrators derive in a system of collective violence is usually granted directly or indirectly by the instigating elite, who also have the power to disable perpetrators if they so choose and even redefine them as the enemy, thus rendering them potential victims.

An important feature of instigators is that they act as *cata-lyst* of collective violence, often by conveying a vision for a better life or by identifying a perceived source of threat in times of social unrest. . . .

Given their special role in catalyzing social change, instigators tend to be perceived as agents that are less interchangeable than perpetrators. Hence, counter-factual replays of history that undo wars, genocides, or terrorist acts by negating preceding human actions may be more likely to focus on a single instigator than a multitude of perpetrators. For example, the chance that the Holocaust would have been averted if any one of its perpetrators had not existed appears to be dramatically lower than if Hitler had not existed. Put differently, the social influence of instigators and perpetrators is strongly asymmetric: Instigators shape the thinking and guide the behavior of perpetrators, but perpetrators have relatively little influence on the motives or plans of instigators.

At present [2002], the main instigator of terrorism by Islamic militants is Osama bin Laden. Bin Laden is believed to be linked to the September 11 attacks and the current military attacks in Afghanistan are aimed at destroying his terrorist network, al-Qaida ("the base"), which funds and trains terrorists. On February 23, 1998, bin Laden and his associates, under the banner of the World Islamic Front, issued a statement that accused the United States and its allies of crimes against God and Muslims: "All these crimes and sins committed by the Americans are a clear declaration of war on God, his messenger [the prophet Muhammad], and Muslims." The statement—apparently sanctioned by God—calls for a holy war (jihad) against the United States and its allies:

> On that basis, and in compliance with God's order, we issue the following fatwa [religious decree] to all Muslims: The ruling to kill the Americans and their allies—civilians and military—is an individual duty for every Muslim who can do it in any country in which it is possible to do it. . . .

> We—with God's help—call on every Muslim who believes in God and wishes to be rewarded to comply with God's order to kill the Americans and plunder their money wherever and whenever they find it. We also call on Muslim ulema [community], leaders, youths, and soldiers to launch the raid on Satan's U.S. troops and the devil's supporters allying with them, and to displace those who are behind them so that they may learn a lesson.

That bin Laden envisions himself as an instigator of collective violence was made clear in a *Time* interview on December 23, 1998. When asked whether he was responsible for the bomb attacks on two American embassies in Africa, bin Laden stated in his reply, "Our job is to instigate and, by grace of God, we did that, and certain people responded to this instigation."

According to bin Laden, "hostility toward America is a religious duty, and we hope to be rewarded for it by God." The reframing of calls for violence as "duties" or "moral obligations" is a popular technique of instigators to legitimize collective violence. By linking the perpetration of terrorism to a religious duty, bin Laden uses God as the ultimate authority. In effect, bin Laden has claimed that if you fail to try to kill Americans, you have failed in your duty to God. Such messages can instill powerful feelings of moral obligation to an ideal or cause. . . .

Instigators Propagate Nationalism

Like other instigators of collective violence, bin Laden has garnered support by using nationalism—in this case, religious nationalism—to incite hatred against a "common enemy." On the one hand, nationalism creates an egotistic sense of in-group cohesion by emphasizing the shared greatness of a people. According to bin Laden, only Muslims—indeed only Muslims that follow his call to violence—are worthy in God's eyes. The message conveyed is that only compliant Muslims are worthy of moral treatment. . . .

Exiled al Qaida leader Osama bin Laden in Afghanistan talks during a television interview in April 1998. AP Images.

On the other hand, nationalism can exacerbate feelings of threat by pointing to the nation's precariousness, feelings of hatred by pointing to those deemed responsible for its hardships and failures, and feelings of insult due to the belief that one's nation has not received the respect it deserves. . . .

The Nazi image of a German master race threatened by an international Jewish plague illustrates the point. For bin Laden, the U.S. military presence on Islamic holy land is an act of U.S. "Crusader" aggression. He has repeatedly mentioned the importance of destroying the myth of the American superpower. For instance, in the aforementioned *Time* interview, bin Laden stated, "I am confident that Muslims will be able to end the legend of the so-called superpower that is America."

Nationalism plays upon a fundamental aspect of human social cognition: the tendency to categorize individuals into groups. Even when the basis of social categorization is trivial, people tend to discriminate in favor of ingroup members and against outgroup members. Nationalism is particularly effective at creating a strong sense of *us* versus *them* because nations (unlike states) tend to be defined in terms of features that are of high personal and social importance, such as ethnicity, race, religion, ideology, and language. Consequently, the nation may be perceived, and may in fact behave, not merely as an aggregate but as a cohesive *entity*.

In bin Laden's case, the ingroup is "the Islamic nation or God's children" (i.e., Muslims) and the outgroup, "God's enemies" (i.e., non-Muslims, but especially Jews and powerful Christians, like the Americans). In his August 23, 1996, "Declaration of War Against the Americans Who Occupy the Land of the Two Holy Mosques," bin Laden called for "a guerilla war, where the sons of the nation, and not the military forces, take part in it." Bin Laden's use of language is also aimed at dehumanizing the citizens of the United States and its allied countries by labeling them as "infidels" or "devil's supporters." This use of labeling is reminiscent of Hitler's labeling of Jews as vermin, bacilli, and "kikes." . . . The response by the Bush administration has also tended to vilify the other side, albeit with more qualification than bin Laden has been willing to grant.

Vilification and Attribution of Evil

The escalation of the conflict triggered by the September 11 attacks—the "war on terrorism," as it is being called—owes much to the attribution of evil by both sides. The Bush administration has repeatedly couched the present conflict as one between the forces of good and evil, much as bin Laden has done. For instance, in his address to the nation on September 11, Bush repeatedly referred to evil: "Thousands of lives were suddenly ended by evil, despicable acts of terror," "Today, our nation saw evil," "The search is underway for those who are behind these evil acts." In the same address, Bush quoted Psalm 23: "Even though I walk through the valley of the shadow of death, I fear no evil, for You are with me." The day after the terrorist attacks, Bush stated, "This will be a monumental struggle of good versus evil. But good will prevail." On September 26, in another press release, Bush reiterated, "We must never forget this will be a long struggle, that there are evil people in the world who hate America. And we won't relent." At present, then, the leaders of both sides of this conflict have presented it in simplistic terms as a "struggle of good versus evil." This totalistic portrayal, emphasizing an "us" and "them," can heighten social identification and outgroup derogation and steer people toward supporting an escalation of violence. . . .

Attributions of evil are a natural response to intentional attack, especially when it is construed as unprovoked. But citizens and leaders alike ought to be cognizant of the behavioral effects that such construals may have. We are in the midst of an international conflict that has the potential to escalate, and we need to be on guard against vilification, totalistic thinking, and hubristic responses that prompt further violence at the same time that we guard ourselves against terrorism, because both pose a real threat to our security and chances for prosperity.

Young Males' Attraction to Risk Makes Them Prime Recruits in the War on Terror

Cheryl Benard

Cheryl Benard, a political scientist, is director of the Rand Corporation's Initiative for Middle Eastern Youth and the author of Civil Democratic Islam.

In the following essay, Cheryl Benard finds that the slow maturation of the male brain and the large percentage of the Middle Eastern population under the age of nineteen have significant implications for the war on terror. She cites recent studies that show that before the age of twenty-two to twenty-four, young men are inclined to seek out risk and excitement while overestimating their own abilities and underestimating the potential for danger. This is consistent with the reality that in Muslim communities, it is young men who most frequently engage in violent behavior. By the same token, the U.S. Army recruits primarily teenagers. The war on terror would look very different if it were not fought by teenagers on both sides, Benard claims.

About the time of Easter . . . , many thousands of boys, ranging in age from six years to full maturity, left the plows or carts which they were driving, the flocks which they were pasturing, and anything else which they were doing . . . [and] put up banners and began to journey to Jerusalem. . . . They [said] that they were equal to the Divine will in this matter and that, whatever God might wish to do with them, they would accept it willingly and with humble spirit. Some were turned back at Metz, others at Piacenza, and even others at Rome. Still others got to Marseilles, but whether they

Cheryl Benard, "Toy Soldiers: The Youth Factor in the War on Terror," *Current History*, vol. 106, no. 696, January 2007, pp. 27–30. Copyright © 2009 by Current History, Inc. Reproduced by permission of *Current History Magazine.*

crossed to the Holy Land or what their end was is uncertain. One thing is sure: that of the many thousands who rose up, only very few returned.

—From a description of the so-called Children's Crusade
in *Chronica Regiae Coloniensis Continuatio prima*,
translated by James Brundage

Much has been made of an ominous demographic reality prevalent in the Middle East. Although the exact number varies from country to country, any speaker who mentions the proportion of the population below age 20, or below age 16, can count on receiving gasps of surprise from Western audiences. Fifty percent of the population below age 19! Sixty-five percent below age 25! And no functioning economy to absorb them. It is clear even to a layperson that this spells trouble.

Experts will point out that it could also spell prosperity—in theory. In theory, a young population has the potential to be productive and to bless its society with a low dependency ratio: that is, with a larger segment of productive workers supporting a smaller segment of the elderly, the very young, the incapacitated, and otherwise nonproductive individuals who must count on tapping into the income of others. In reality, though, cultural, political, and economic factors can—and throughout much of the Islamic world do—stand in the way of productivity and prosperity. The youth overhang, instead of constituting a motor for growth, becomes what Isobel Coleman of the Council on Foreign Relations has called a potential "youthquake" and a "massive demographic tsunami."

Many young people in the Middle East, especially the famously more volatile young males, are deprived of sensible activities, bereft of real hope for a happy and independent future, unschooled in practical modes of thinking, and sexually frustrated in their strict and puritanical societies. Many are hammered with the rousing appeals of radical preachers and ideologues. Others are simply bored and purposeless. Clearly this is not a promising recipe for stable social advancement.

All of these social conditions and their implications in the region are being discussed and fretted over, and with good cause. But another variable in the situation has received less attention: the underlying mindset and mental development of young adults generally. I would argue that, beneath many of the conflicts tearing at the Middle East today, including the war on terror, the Palestinian intifada against Israel and the "Insurgency" in Iraq—as indeed underneath probably most instances of major violence throughout history—there lies an unspoken, disturbing social contract in which older people pursue agendas by deploying the volatile weapon of mentally not-yet mature younger men.

The Immature Brain

While this issue has important ethical dimensions, the question is raised more neutrally by recent neurological and developmental findings that in turn are the product of improved medical technology. Increasingly sophisticated Magnetic Resonance Imaging (MRI) of brains, in combination with research in experimental psychology, indicates that maturation may take place more gradually and conclude later than formerly presumed. A number of studies suggest that mental and behavioral development continues to be in considerable flux until somewhere between the ages of 22 and 24; that before this time, young people and particularly young men are inclined to show particular responses, behaviors, and mindsets; and that these are of high relevance to their own personal safety and well-being and to those of others around them.

The findings can be summed up as follows: young men are strongly inclined to seek out situations of risk, excitement, and danger; and they also are likely to make fallacious judgments about their own abilities, overestimating their capacities and underestimating objective obstacles and dangers. In a variety of important interactive contexts, as a result, their reactions predictably veer toward the impulsive taking of unwise risks. All of this affects their ability not so much to understand, but to process and "believe in" the potential for negative outcomes and even catastrophic consequences of their decisions.

Not much of this, of course, really comes as a surprise. That young people are impulsive and that young men like to test themselves in situations of high risk is well known. Recent research, however, provides a much more specific window into the mechanics of youthful responses and decisions, as well as the situations that represent a particular risk for reactions that can be harmful to the individual or to others. It also reveals the inherence of some of these behaviors, which are not individual failings or errors but flow from a natural developmental process to which all individuals are subject—and which others might exploit.

The first conclusion that suggests itself from current research in neurological development is that adolescence and young adulthood conclude later than formerly assumed. Brain development is of course an ongoing process. Adolescence, however, is a time of particularly high change. Longitudinal studies following changes in the prefrontal cortex indicate that the changes do not wind down until age 22 or even later. The prefrontal cortex is jovially referred to by experts in this field as the "area of sober second thought." This is the part of the mind that carefully considers the consequences of a decision, weighs the pros and cons, reflects, and, depending on the evidence, may come to reconsider. In the absence of a fully developed prefrontal cortex, an individual will be more inclined to follow through on a spontaneous, impulsive decision.

In a 2004 study titled "Adolescent Brain Development and Drug Abuse," Ken Winters of the University of Minnesota noted that three brain structures that undergo maturation during youth—the nucleus accumbens, amygdale, and prefrontal cortex—have important implications for understanding adolescent behavior. "An immature nucleus accumbens is believed to result in preferences for activities that require low effort yet produce high excitement. . . . The amygdale is the structure responsible for integrating emotional reactions to pleasurable and aversive experiences. It is believed that a developing amygdale contributes to two behavioral effects: the tendency for adolescents to react explosively to situations rather than with more controlled responses, and the propensity for youth to misread neutral or inquisitive facial expressions of others as a sign of anger. And one of the last areas to mature is the prefrontal cortex . . . responsible for the complex processing of information, ranging from making judgments to controlling impulses, foreseeing consequences, and setting goals and plans. An immature prefrontal cortex is thought to be the neurobiological explanation for why teenagers show poor judgment and too often act before they think."

Recent MRI and brain mapping research has also focused on the cerebellum, a part of the brain formerly thought to relate primarily to physical movement, but now found to coordinate a variety of cognitive processes and to enable individuals to "navigate" social life. As Jay Giedd of the National Institute of Mental Health, among others, has pointed out, this portion of the brain is not fully developed until well into the early twenties.

Besides magnetic resonance imaging, a second strand of research employs experiments to measure the responses and the decision making of individuals in relation to an assortment of variables, among them, age and gender. These include tests that place an individual in simulated decision-making scenarios, such as a driving situation in which he or she must make a split-second decision on whether or not to proceed through an intersection; tests that require the individual to override a physical reflex, for example by deliberately not looking in the direction of a suddenly bright light; gambling tasks that measure risk aversion; and many more. Young men perform very poorly on all of these tasks.

Thrill Seekers

In turn, outcomes suggested by the findings of both of these research methods are reflected in broader social data. Changes that begin with adolescence and conclude at the end of young adulthood incline young people, and young men in particular, to seek excitement, to misjudge situations, and to dismiss danger. These inclinations are clearly readable in morbidity rates, which increase by a dramatic 200 to 300 percent between childhood and full adulthood. . . .

Roadside accidents, for example, are one arena in which this plays itself out. In a 2005 study commissioned by the Allstate Foundation, accident fatalities and car-related injuries to young drivers were studied in collaboration with Temple University, which brought neuropsychiatric and experimental findings to bear in an analysis of accident causation. The study noted that "key parts of the brain's decision-making circuitry do not fully develop until the mid-20s. So, in actual driving situations, teens may weigh the consequences of unsafe driving quite differently than adults do. This, combined with the increased appetite for novelty and sensation that most teens experience at the onset of puberty, makes teens more disposed to risk-taking behind the wheel—often with deadly results.

Males below the age of 24 have nearly three times as many accidents as their older counterparts; their accidents are significantly more likely to be fatal; and accident analysis reveals that the young men are almost always at fault. This is not attributable, as some might suppose, to a lack of experience or technical skill. Rather, the problem lies in the propensity of young men to take risks, to misjudge or ignore danger, and to make erroneous split-second decisions on the basis of factually unwarranted optimism and overconfidence. Young people are also substantially more likely to make the decision to drive while under the influence of alcohol or drugs.

The Allstate study found that conventional drivers' education programs are not effective in countering these dangerous youthful inclinations. They can enhance skill levels and convey information, including warnings about dangers and advice about safer decisions, but they do not affect the underlying impulses and motivations. Interestingly, the expedient of placing a female passenger in the vehicle with the young male driver effects more improvement in safe driving than a lecture or a class. Having him joined by another young male, on the other hand, will increase the likelihood of reckless driving.

Membership in a clandestine terrorist cell; online linkages with glamorous, dangerous individuals; the opportunity to belong to a feared and seemingly heroic movement complete with martyrs—all of this is inherently appealing to young people.

Another example of how young adulthood differs from both childhood and full adulthood can be found in recent research on Post Traumatic Stress Disorder—in particular, a study published in the October 2006 issue of the American Journal of Psychiatry. Research conducted at Walter Reed Army Medical Hospital on veterans of combat in Afghanistan and Iraq found that soldiers below age 25 are 3.4 times more likely to experience Post Traumatic Stress Disorder than older soldiers. This is in accordance with other research showing adolescence and young adulthood are a time of particular vulnerability to stress, and an age at which grief and loss are felt with enhanced severity.

A few caveats are in order before speculating on the political significance of these insights into young people's mentality. First, this research is fairly young and we may come, at some future point, to challenge or even reverse its findings. Second, the determinism of responses and behaviors varies. The mere fact that inclinations or reflexes push an individual in a certain direction does not mean that he or she is unable to override them; it just means that this may be more difficult.

Finally, the point being made by the research is that maturation is a process. The findings do not mean that individuals are irresponsible and volatile until, at some arbitrary point, be it 18 or 21 or 22 or 24, they suddenly emerge as mature and sober adults. Maturation unfolds at different rates and to different degrees; it seems reasonable to presume, though this has not yet been studied, that much will also depend on the surrounding societal circumstances, on education, and on other variables affecting the life circumstances and influences operating on the individual young adult.

It remains nonetheless a telling fact that, within the Middle East and Muslim communities worldwide, young males constitute the most numerous participants in violent behavior and pose the greatest security threat to Western societies. Indeed, Western European security agencies report that radicalization among European Muslim minority communities is manifesting itself at ever-younger ages, with 14 and 15 now the typical age at which young people are drawn into extremism. (The most effective recruiting tool today is the Internet.)

It is not difficult to see that propensities inherent in this age group, and effective until age 24 or so, make this subpopulation an ideal audience for radical recruitment. Membership in a clandestine terrorist cell; online linkages with glamorous, dangerous individuals; the opportunity to belong to a feared and seemingly heroic movement complete with martyrs—all of this is inherently appealing to young people. And membership comes with flaming speeches, weapons, facemasks, and all the accoutrements of a forbidden armed struggle. Better-adjusted male teenagers satisfy their craving for excitement with video games; those who belong to a disaffected minority may be drawn, at least in some instances, to the real thing.

How Real Is Real?

After all, when you are an adolescent, how real is real? The question cannot yet be scientifically measured, but we can glimpse an answer in some of the Muslim suicide bomber videos circulating on the Internet. Do not look, for the moment, at the chanting group of celebrants surrounding the prospective bomber. Ignore the splendid, resolute text he is reading from his notes. Look instead at his face, and take note of the momentary expression of surprise, even shock. Did this young man, when he signed up to become a suicide bomber, truly understand that this moment would come, that it would feel like this, that it would be real and irreversible? His expression suggests otherwise but there is no turning back, not with the video camera rolling and his cheering comrades ready to pack him into the truck—where in many cases, to strengthen his resolve, he will be handcuffed to the steering wheel.

Similarly, the teenagers who place improvised explosive devices (IEDS) on the streets of Baghdad may not have thought very far beyond the money, or the approbation of their clique, with which this act is rewarded. US intelligence officers report seeing children, including a 14-year-old girl, placing roadside IEDS. Iraqi officials report capturing near the Syrian border a 10-year-old boy who had "come to wage jihad."

Better-adjusted male teenagers satisfy their craving for excitement with video games; those who belong to a disaffected minority may be drawn, at least in some instances, to the real thing.

This is not to dismiss the more elaborate, complex approaches that are being put forward to explain and respond to the threat of Islamist radicalism, global terrorism, and the insurgency in Iraq. Certainly, political and ideological and cultural and ethnic and economic and perhaps religious reasons play a part. But with all of that, it would be a mistake to forget that most of the minds involved are very young and acting on impulses and a logic that any proposed solutions should take into account.

It is necessary to mention, as well, that the same is true on the other side of this conflict. If America's adversaries in Iraq, for example, are primarily young, then so are the soldiers that the United States is sending forward to confront them. There is some difficulty in criticizing Islamist recruitment videos aimed at teenage viewers, when the online game "America's Army" similarly seeks to rope in 14-year-olds for subsequent service. This multiplayer interactive online game is a recruiting tool created by the US military. It is popular because of its excellent graphics and because it is free. Research conducted by the US military shows that the game is instrumental in the decision of numerous young people to join the actual armed services.

The point here obviously is not to equate the goal of these two "recruiting agencies." The point is that 14-year-old males are largely vulnerable to the promise of thrills and danger and largely oblivious to risk, and that—if the research cited above is correct—they will not have changed enough by 17 or 18 years of age to assure that their decision to join a war and risk death and dismemberment has been judicious, thoughtful, and taken in full understanding of what it can entail. Research on young people's brain development also implies that militaries ought, at a minimum, to consider some of the revealed inclinations and predispositions of young adults in their training and deployment of younger soldiers. Thus, a propensity to interpret facial expressions as reflecting hostility can clearly be detrimental in interactions with civilian populations, for example in house searches.

More generally, developmental research raises provocative questions for a US intervention in Iraq in which the largest proportion of casualties is borne by troops aged 21 and below.

Do optimistic risk assessments and split-second decisions in favor of the more dangerous path play a role? Does the United States really have a "volunteer army" if very young adults have an impaired ability to judge the consequences of their decisions? And perhaps most intriguingly of all: What would the "war on terror" look like if neither side could deploy large numbers of young men with high affect, operating on hair-trigger responses, and low on "sober second thought"?

Survivor Makes Aggression Attractive

Christine McGovern

Christine McGovern is the dean of faculty at Georgetown Visitation Preparatory School in Washington, D.C.

Christine McGovern is concerned in the following article that the popularity of the television show Survivor *will have an impact on her teaching of* Lord of the Flies. *In the eleven years that she has taught the novel, her students are cooperative, courageous, and selfless when placed in a simulated survival setting. When they read* Lord of the Flies, *they are shocked by the behavior of the children. With the experience of* Survivor, *however, where greed, duplicity, and concern only for self are rewarded, she wonders if her students will behave differently and approach the book differently.*

One of the great joys of teaching ninth grade literature is in serious jeopardy now that "Survivor" has crept into our national consciousness. No longer will my students become acquainted with the "darkness of man's heart" through William Golding's *Lord of the Flies*. Thanks to [the] television phenomenon, man's-inhumanity-to-man will seem old hat—or will it?

A Lesson in Survival

For 11 years, I have taught the novel to freshmen at Georgetown Visitation, a Catholic girls' school here in D.C. The journey is rough, so I begin with a pre-reading activity. I tell them: Your plane has crashed on a desert island which has a mountainous area, a forest, a sandy beach and a lagoon. All adults have perished. The plane has drifted out to sea. You have only the items on your person and the clothes on your back. Your job is to organize to survive.

I then retreat to the corner of the room and record what happens next. After witnessing this exercise more than 30 times, I never fail to be amazed by the students' resourcefulness. Usually they, like the boys in the novel, elect a leader who organizes them into work groups to feed, shelter, and sometimes entertain, each other.

Their concerns mirror the boys' on the island as they plan for basic survival and rescue. They build a fire for warmth, protection, and roasting interesting flora and fauna. Only once did they attempt to cook one of their own.

Mostly they work cooperatively—a characteristic some label as a "feminine" value. Sometimes they follow their leader while other times the leader is usurped by a power-hungry rival. Occasionally a small band will break off from the group, bored or overwhelmed by the chaos of the classroom/island.

They tend to injuries, personal hygiene, and once in a while they even say a prayer to stave off any "beasts" who might attack them at night.

Danger and fear emerge early on, foreshadowing the evil that lurks in the hearts of the characters and themselves. All sorts of monsters invade their paradise, but usually they fend off the aggressor.

Only once has a class succeeded in getting off the island. Pooling their talents, they made a "boat" from desks with a sail made by linking their plaid uniform kilts and moved their vessel at full mast toward the door and safety.

Evil Comes as a Surprise

The results of the exercise almost always reinforce the virtues of selflessness, courage, teamwork, and kindness. So, they are in for a surprise when the characters rebel from rules and even plot to kill each other.

Susan Hawk, Rudy Boesch, Richard Hatch, and Kelly Wiglesworth at the Survivor *party in Los Angeles on August 23, 2000.* Kevin Winter/Getty Images.

Now having met the evil Richard, vengeful Sue, and traitorous Kelly [contestants on the first *Survivor*] I'm not sure they will believe that savagery, if left unchecked, is a bad thing. Worse, I fear that they will identify the television show with the novel. Richard becomes the choirboy-turned-murderer, Jack. The revulsion against rat cuisine replaces reluctance to eat raw pig meat, and the $1 million pot of gold seems a far more desirable reward than the triumph of virtue.

However, I have been assured by my sophomores, who read *Lord of the Flies* untainted by "Survivor," that the novel's impact will not suffer by comparison. Yes, they say, students may foresee a breakdown in society sooner as alliances forge enmities. Yes, they might recognize earlier the danger of peer pressure to betray their friends. But, no, human beings can still tell the difference between a hoked-up TV show and a fictional life-and-death situation with no escape hatch.

I'm not so sure. Golding's title, *Lord of the Flies*, refers to the ancient Hebrew name for the Devil. And the Devil is a snake. And the snake ate the rat.

Alienation from Peers Can Lead Teens to Violence

Antonius H.N. Cillessen

Antonius H.N. Cillessen is a professor of developmental psychology at Radboud Universiteit Nijmegen in The Netherlands.

In the following essay, Antonius H.N. Cillessen suggests that while a certain level of conflict with peers is a normal part of teenage life, more serious forms of teenage violence have recently emerged, such as school shootings. He cites studies that indicate that teens involved in more serious violence were motivated by factors within their peer group. Additionally, the violent teens were perceived as outsiders within this peer group. Teenagers who are on the outside of their peer group may get frustrated, he reports, and this frustration can turn into violence if these teenagers have certain risk factors. Among these risk factors are poor anger management skills, ready access to weapons, few meaningful friendships, and a distorted view of society.

Violence among children and youth is a serious concern, as evidenced by the intense media coverage of incidents such as the school shootings at Columbine High School in Littleton, Colo., on Apr. 20, 1999. Occurrences such as these that have taken place in relatively well-to-do areas in usually quiet small towns defy the stereotype that locates juvenile violent behavior in poor inner-city neighborhoods, and have brought teenage violence closer to home for many Americans.

Such incidents clearly differ from the phenomena that are more common in the peer group. A certain amount of disagreement and mutual conflict with peers is expected among

Antonius H.N. Cillessen, "Understanding the Predictors of Violent Adolescent Behavior," *USA Today Magazine*, vol. 130, no. 2684, May 2002, pp. 48–49. Copyright © 2002 Society for the Advancement of Education. Reproduced by permission.

adolescents. To disagree with others who have different opinions or preferences is a normal aspect of the emergence of self-awareness and the development of a sense of one's uniqueness and identity. In the same way that differences of opinion and disagreements with adults are a normal part of adolescence, those with peers are a normative part of adolescent development.

If they are intense, these forms of adolescent conflict may lead to a physical fight, or they might be expressed in more relational forms of aggression, such as spreading a rumor about another person or excluding someone from a group or group activity. Although these forms of aggression should not be condoned, the question here is what personal or situational factors cause adolescents to cross the line between these "ordinary" forms of aggression and the serious, destructive, and unconscionable forms of aggression that have been witnessed recently.

Outsiders More Likely to Become Violent

Over the last two decades, the study of violence and aggression has received an increasing amount of attention from behavioral scientists, partly in response to the rising number of incidents among children and youth. However, a new and disturbing element has been added to the phenomenon of juvenile violence, with recent incidents being more deadly than before and spreading to settings where they have not typically been expected.

Based on anecdotal evidence presented in the media, including interviews with at-risk adolescents who were prevented from committing serious crimes by school counselors who recognized the warning signals these youths gave, two things are clear. First, teen violence is embedded in the context of the peer group. Many of the recent school shootings were committed by friends, and the violence often seemed to take place in response to certain stressors within the peer group. Second, evidence suggests that the students involved in high school shootings were more likely to be outsiders or victims of aggression by peers rather than aggressive bullies. Typically, they were individuals on the fringe of the peer group who felt excluded, alienated, and victimized. This defeats the stereotype of the aggressive, antisocial individual as the one most likely to commit such serious crimes.

The dynamics of the adolescent peer group are more subtle than is commonly assumed. Complex processes in the group reinforce or influence the occurrence of antisocial behavior The stereotypical perception is that aggressive students are generally disliked, rejected by peers, and friendless. Actually, this is only partly true. While there is a relationship between being aggressive and being rejected by peers, another process has been documented by several researchers.

Philip Rodkin of the University of Illinois has demonstrated that adolescent boys who are perceived as popular in the peer group can be divided into two subgroups. One, the "model boys," consists of those who are prosocial, empathic to the needs of others, and positive in their interactions with peers. The second, the "tough boys," consists of those whose profile is a mix of positive and negative behaviors. They are liked by some of their peers, but disliked by others. Most importantly, while these boys have many social skills, they also use aggressive tactics to maintain their reputation in the peer group.

Kathryn LaFontana of Sacred Heart University [in Fairfield, Connecticut] has corroborated the idea that there is a relationship between popularity and aggressiveness, especially in adolescent groups. She has found that the way children and adolescents perceive popular peers is not unequivocally positive, but again a mixture of positive and negative elements. Children perceive peers who are labeled as "popular" as cooperative and prosocial, but also as aggressive and manipulative in their social relationships with others. The investigations by

Rodkin, LaFontana, and others reveal the Machiavellian [ruthlessly manipulative] nature of the members of the "popular crowd" in adolescent groups. They are very socially skilled people who know how to make friends and be cooperative, but how to be manipulative as well in order to achieve their goals.

This shows that aggressive and manipulative behavior is an important part of adolescent peer relations, and may be more subtle and pervasive than people tend to believe. Second, aggressive, manipulative, and dominant behavior is not limited to the stereotypical bully, but is a more inclusive, normative, and widespread phenomenon in adolescent peer groups. Third, individuals who are at the periphery of the peer system, who do not have the Machiavellian competence to "fit in" may be the individuals who are the most likely to get frustrated. If they have poor anger control, distorted views about themselves or society, lack the friendships or peer interactions in which they can test their views against reality, and have access to and experience with the use of weapons, a deadly mix may be created.

Beyond the anecdotal evidence presented in the media, what does research reveal about the predictors of the complex dynamics of adolescent peer relations? Before discussing the specific predictors of adolescent aggression, several methodological points need to be made.

First, statistically speaking, prediction of exceptional behavior is difficult. Because it is not often observable, it is hard to collect enough data to forecast the next occurrence. The consequences of each occurrence of teenage violence are devastating and their absolute frequency has increased sharply. Yet, their relative frequency is still low compared to the fact that millions of students have relatively normal school days most of the year. . . .

Predictive Risk Factors

What, then, is known about the concurrent correlates and early predictors of teenage violence? Five sets of variables are discussed below. This list is not necessarily comprehensive, but summarizes a set of factors that has been considered frequently in recent research.

- There is evidence for reciprocity of aggressive behavior. This means that individuals who engage in aggressive behavior tend to be the targets or victims of aggression by others as well. This finding has emerged at various levels of analyses. It appears at the individual level of analysis—that is, children or adolescents who are the targets of aggression by others tend to act aggressively towards their peers in general. Interestingly, the finding also emerges at the dyadic [a group of two] level of analysis. That is to say, if Anthony starts fights with Ben, Ben also starts fights with Anthony. There are multiple reasons for this correlation. Whatever the reasons, it is clear that someone who is the frequent target of aggression by others may develop a tendency to retaliate, either towards specific others or towards the peer group in general.

- A distorted view of the social world is often associated with aggressive behavior. Several studies have shown that rejected-aggressive children are not very accurate perceivers of their behavior in interactions with peers. They often wrongly assume that others have hostile intentions towards them and misperceive the effects their behavior may have on others. It is difficult to determine whether these hostile perceptions cause aggression or whether experiences of aggression (e.g., by an abusive parent or in a violent neighborhood) cause a hostile worldview. There is reason to believe that both processes operate at the same time. . . .

- What is the role of psychopathology in the occurrence of teenage violence? It has sometimes been suggested that aggression in the peer group may primarily be a function of an underlying disturbance, and that the contribution of the group itself is minimal. Most researchers disagree. In various cases of teen violence, the perpetrators were children or adolescents who were often hardly different from others and were not characterized by a serious form of mental illness. They may have felt anger and perceived hostility, but they were not psychotic. Most researchers believe that teenage violence cannot simply be reduced to underlying forms of psychopathology of the individual child or adolescent, but that the processes taking place in peer relationships need to be seriously considered as contributing causes.

- What is the role of parents? Those who monitor their offspring's activities are less likely to have children who get into trouble. Parents can play a positive role via the opportunities they give their children to interact with peers and the feedback they provide to their kids about their choice of friends. Conversely, those who are physically abusive toward their children or each other provide models of aggressive behavior their offspring are likely to imitate. Low parental monitoring of kids' activities and harsh physical punishment predict aggressive behavior by the child. In spite of these causal effects, a tendency to blame only the parents is unjustified. They are just one factor to be considered among the multiple causes of childhood aggression.

- Societal and cultural factors cannot be ignored. Norms have changed and can influence behavior in new ways. Western societies are extremely accepting of violence, as evidenced by the nature and frequency of it youngsters are exposed to by the entertainment industry. Research in psychology clearly indicates that exposure to violence breeds violence. The violence displayed in school shootings hardly differs from what can be observed daily in the media and in computer games. At a more subtle level, our competitive and achievement-oriented society values Machiavellian concepts that benefit the individual at the expense of the community.

In addition, the availability of guns to teenagers remains a serious problem. As indicated, conflicting identities, a lack of mature judgment, and a relative inability to oversee the consequences of one's actions are inherent aspects of this normative human development process called adolescence. Amidst all other predictors of teenage violence, society bears a serious responsibility by allowing adolescents access to guns, with a simple finger movement in an unreflected state of anger or sadness, so common for this age, sufficient to trigger deadly consequences.

Violent Behavior by Teenage Girls Needs to Be Taken Seriously

Georgie Binks

Georgie Binks is a writer living in Toronto. She has written for the Toronto Star, National Post, Globe and Mail, *and* Chatelaine. *She is also a former CBC radio and television reporter and editor.*

In the following viewpoint, Georgie Binks reports that the number of violent acts by teenage girls in Canada jumped by 130 percent from 1988 to 1998 and since then has remained somewhat constant at five thousand to six thousand per year. She claims there are numerous reasons why girls become violent. Some have low self-esteem and fall into a violent peer group. Others come from a violent background. Additionally, Binks maintains, the media have been guilty of glamorizing female violence.

[In March 2006], five Manitoba girls attacked a teacher's aide, beating her with a flashlight. A school principal and teachers were punched and hit as they tried to intervene.

Teachers and the community have been shocked by the attack. It's not the first time we've heard about girls turning violent. There was the terrible murder of Reena Virk, 14, beaten and drowned in 1997 on Vancouver Island. The attack was committed by a group that included teenaged girls.

Is there actually an increase in violent acts committed by teenaged girls these days? And if so, what are the reasons, and are we dealing with it?

Reasons for Girl Violence

In the 10 years leading up to 1998, there was a steady and significant increase in girl violence—it jumped by nearly 130 per cent. Then, according to the Canadian Centre for Justice Statistics, from 1999–2004 the total number of violent attacks (murder, assault, robbery) by girls stabilized at approximately 5,000 to 6,000 a year. The numbers are one-third of what they are for boys. Still, they are disturbing.

It's not surprising in a world whose mantra has been "Girl Power" ever since the Spice Girls popularized it that young females are taking matters into their own hands.

Simon Fraser [University] psychology professor, Marlene Moretti, lead investigator on the Gender and Aggression Project for the Canadian Institutes of Health Research, cautions that: "There are programs aimed at teaching girls to be assertive, to believe in themselves, have a sense of self-esteem and not allow themselves to be pushed around or intimidated or drawn into a peer group.

"That's great if it's done appropriately. However, some families don't understand the difference between aggression and assertiveness."

There's no simple reason girls become aggressive and violent. Moretti says, "One size doesn't fit all. There are marginalized girls with low self-esteem who fall into the wrong crowd and become aggressive. They are girls who are both victimized and bullied by others. Then there are girls who are popular and are very oppressive—those girls often grow out of it."

Rebecca Godfrey, author of *Under the Bridge: The True Story of the Murder of Reena Virk*, learned a lot about violent girls when covering the trials of those charged in Virk's murder.

She says, "A lot of these girls came from violent environments. The fathers of two of the girls had been murdered and they were in very violent situations. There was nobody who came through for them, like a social worker or a program.

Kelly Ellard, seventeen, on March 10, 2000. She is on trial for the beating death of fourteen-year-old Reena Virk. Ms. Ellard is accused along with six other girls and one boy, all aged between fourteen and sixteen. Don MacKinnon/Getty Images.

The pop culture they were interested in was glorified violence, which influenced their sense of what was glamourous and powerful."

The Media Plays a Role

The media definitely plays its part in glamourizing tough girls. Think of the women in the *Charlie's Angels* movies taking down their opponents or *Kill Bill*'s Uma Thurman meting out justice. Tough girls kick ass, right?

Moretti says if a girl doesn't have a lot to hang onto, images like these convey the message that this is a great way to be respected.

Of course, with female violence, as with just about everything else female these days, it's become sexualized. Think of the *Seinfeld* episode where Jerry drooled over thoughts of a "catfight."

When you combine these images with girls who already are dealing with the pressures of puberty you can easily create a ticking time bomb.

"Girls are already under pressure as they enter adolescence. They're competing for social status, and trying to be attractive. Wanting to feel part of a group, they can drift into groups of girls where they feel they can compete. Often that means being involved in aggressive behaviour with each other," Moretti says.

In his book *See Jane Hit* James Garbarino praises the physical outlet that sports has given girls for their energy and aggression, which he views as a positive thing. However, sports cultivates physicality that could translate into physical aggression, he says.

Still, the benefits outweigh the risks. Girls feeling good about themselves on a soccer field usually aren't the same girls angrily beating up another girl in the playground.

The other day I spoke with a teenaged girl who had fans cheering in the bleachers last year as she stood her ground in a fist fight with a male hockey player. However, a five-minute penalty for both players is certainly not what would happen in real life. When confronted with a female who wanted to settle things physically over a guy, the reality of possible assault charges and a fight with no hockey gear convinced that same girl that walking away was the best solution.

Boys are taught how to fight fair and are also cautioned about the implications. Godfrey says girls aren't that familiar with the rules of fighting.

"Boys know you only do one on one, and girls simply go wild. With the Reena Virk case, these same girls had attacked another girl several weeks before in a similar way, setting her hair on fire. In this attack, one of the girls was a kickboxer. You wouldn't have seen that 20 years ago."

Right now, the first step is to take the issue seriously. Godfrey maintains that, "Anything about teenaged girls seems to be trivialized and sexualized, and it shouldn't be."

Violence among teenage girls isn't sexy or funny or cool. But until society starts seeing that, it's going to be pretty difficult to deal with it.

For Further Discussion

1. Paula Alida Roy writes that the island in *Lord of the Flies* is a "boys' club" where the absence of girls symbolizes the dangers of ultramasculinity. What do you think would have happened if there had also been some girls on the island? Why? What would have happened if there had been only girls on the island? Why?

2. Patrick Reilly claims there is no happy ending or anything optimistic about *Lord of the Flies*. What do you think happens to the boys when they leave the island?

3. Paul Slayton describes how Jack and the choirboys become more violent in the course of the novel. At first Jack is reluctant to kill the sow, but doing so makes it easier for them to hunt and slaughter other children. In contemporary society, are people exposed to things that make them more prone to violence? Explain.

4. English teacher Christine McGovern has been teaching *Lord of the Flies* for a number of years and worries that the popularity of the television show *Survivor* will change her students' attitudes toward the book. What similarities do you see between the children in *Lord of the Flies* and the contestants on *Survivor*? What differences?

5. Diane Andrews Henningfeld writes that *Lord of the Flies* is a political allegory, written at a time when the democratic free world of Western Europe and the United States was engaged in a duel with the Iron Curtain countries of Communist Eastern Europe and the Soviet Union. If Golding were writing a political allegory today, who would the likely opponents be? Would there be a war going on in the background? How would it be fought? What would be some of the differences in the plot?

For Further Reading

R.M. Ballantyne, *The Coral Island*. London: T. Nelson, 1858.

Anthony Burgess, *A Clockwork Orange*. London: William Heinemann, 1962.

Daniel Defoe, *Robinson Crusoe*. London: W. Taylor, 1719.

William Golding, *Free Fall*. London: Faber & Faber, 1959; New York: Harcourt, Brace & World, 1960.

———, *Pincher Martin*. London: Faber & Faber, 1956; New York: Capricorn, 1956.

———, *The Pyramid*. London: Faber & Faber, 1967; New York: Harcourt, Brace & World, 1967.

———, *Rites of Passage*. London: Faber & Faber, 1980; New York: Farrar, Straus & Giroux, 1980.

———, *The Spire*. London: Faber & Faber, 1964; New York: Harcourt, Brace & World, 1964.

S.E. Hinton, *Tex*. New York: Delacorte, 1979.

Ken Kesey, *One Flew over the Cuckoo's Nest*. New York: New American Library, 1962.

George Orwell, *Animal Farm*. New York: Harcourt, Brace, Jovanovich, 1946.

———, *1984*. New York: Harcourt, Brace, Jovanovich, 1949.

John Steinbeck, *Of Mice and Men*. New York: Modern Library, 1937.

Johan David Wyss, *The Swiss Family Robinson*. London: M.J. Godwin, 1818.

Bibliography

Books

Howard S. Babb	*The Novels of William Golding.* Columbus: Ohio State University Press, 1970.
James R. Baker	*William Golding: A Critical Study.* New York: St. Martin's Press, 1965.
James R. Baker, ed.	*Critical Essays on William Golding.* Boston: G.K. Hall, 1988.
Lawrence S. Friedman	*William Golding.* New York: Continuum, 1993.
James Gindin	*William Golding.* New York: St. Martin's Press, 1988.
Leighton Hodson	*William Golding.* Edinburgh: Oliver and Boyd, 1969.
Samuel Hynes	*William Golding.* New York: Columbia University Press, 1964.
Arnold Johnston	*Of Earth and Darkness: The Novels of William Golding.* Columbia: University of Missouri Press, 1980.
Mark Kinkead-Weekes and Ian Gregor	*William Golding: A Critical Study.* London: Faber & Faber, 1967.

Marilyn D. McShane and Frank P. Williams III	*Youth Violence and Delinquency: Monsters and Myths.* Westport, CT: Praeger, 2007.
Richard Mizen and Mark Morris	*On Aggression and Violence: An Analytic Perspective.* New York: Palgrave Macmillan, 2007.
Kathryn Seifert	*How Children Become Violent: Keeping Your Kids Out of Gangs, Terrorist Organizations, and Cults.* Boston: Acanthus, 2006.

Periodicals

John W. Aldridge	"Mr. Golding's Own Story," *New York Times Book Review*, December 10, 1961.
Allan Back	"Thinking Clearly About Violence," *Philosophical Studies*, vol. 117, 2004.
Charles Colson	"How Evil Became Cool," *Christianity Today*, August 9, 1999.
C.B. Cox	Review of *Lord of the Flies*, *Critical Quarterly*, Summer 1960.
Bulent Diken and Carsten Bagge Laustsen	"From War to War: *Lord of the Flies* as the Sociology of Spite," *Alternatives: Global, Local, Political*, October–December 2006.
Maurice Dolbier	"Running J.D. Salinger a Close Second," *New York Herald Tribune Books*, May 20, 1962.

Rebecca A. Gellman and Janice L. Delucia-Waack	"Predicting School Violence: A Comparison of Violent and Nonviolent Male Students on Attitudes Toward Violence, Exposure Level to Violence, and PTSD Symptomatology," *Psychology in the Schools*, April 2006.
Victoria Glendinning	"Golding's Voyage Ends Without Landfall," *Observer* (London), June 20, 1993.
Frank Kermode	"The Novels of William Golding," *International Literary Annual*, no. 3, 1961.
NEA Today	"Do Violent Video Games Lead to Aggression?" April 2006.
John Peter	"The Fables of William Golding," *Kenyon Review*, Autumn 1957.
Claire Rosenfield	"'Men of a Smaller Growth': A Psychological Analysis of William Golding's *Lord of the Flies*," *Literature and Psychology*, Autumn 1961.
Henri Talon	"Irony in *Lord of the Flies*," *Essays in Criticism*, July 1968.
Times (London)	"Row over Golding's Nobel Prize," October 7, 1983.
John Wain	"Lord of the Agonies," *Aspect*, April 1963.
Robert J. White	"Butterfly and Beast in *Lord of the Flies*," *Modern Fiction Studies*, Summer 1964.

Index

A

Adolescent males
  aggression of, 116–117
  immature brain development
    in, 167–170, 174
  in Middle East, 166–167
  popularity among, 182–183
  as recruits in war on terror,
    165–175
  thrill seeking by, 170–171
Adult world, 77–78, 80–84, 88–89,
  119
  See also Society
Adventure stories, 133–134
Aggression
  among adolescents, 116–117,
    181–183
  forms of, 181
  instinct for, 75, 78–80
  as response to aggression, 76
  risk factors for, 184–186
Alcott, Louisa May, 35
Aldridge, John, 13
Alienation, 180–186
Allegory
  definition of, 140
  political, 115, 127, 140–141
  psychological, 141–142
  religious, 127–128, 142–143
  social, 122–131
Al-Qaida, 160
Altruism, 80, 110
Anderson, David, 96
Anti-Semitism, 119–120
Aristotle, 36–37
Atomic war, 13, 79, 81, 84

Authoritarianism, 85, 103–104,
  107, 136, 148–149
Authority, 100, 105, 110, 136
Autobiographical elements, 26–27
Automobile accidents, 170–171

B

Baker, James R., 36
Ballantyne, R.M., 23
  See also The Coral Island
  (Ballantyne)
Barbarism. *See* Savagery
Barthes, Roland, 31
Beelzebub, 22, 59, 96, 104–105,
  119
Benard, Cheryl, 165–175
Bierce, Ambrose, 26
Biles, Jack, 34–37
Bill (character), 54, 61
Bin Laden, Osama, 159–163, *162*
Binks, Georgie, 187–191
Biology, 78–81
Bismarck (warship), 12, 21
Blake, William, 26
Boesch, Rudy, *178*
Brain development, 167–170, 174
The Brass Butterfly (Golding), 26
British imperialism, 114
British Royal Navy, 12, 21, 45
Brookfield, Ann. *See* Golding, Ann
The Brothers Karamazov
  (Dostoevsky), 85
Bush, George W., 159, 164